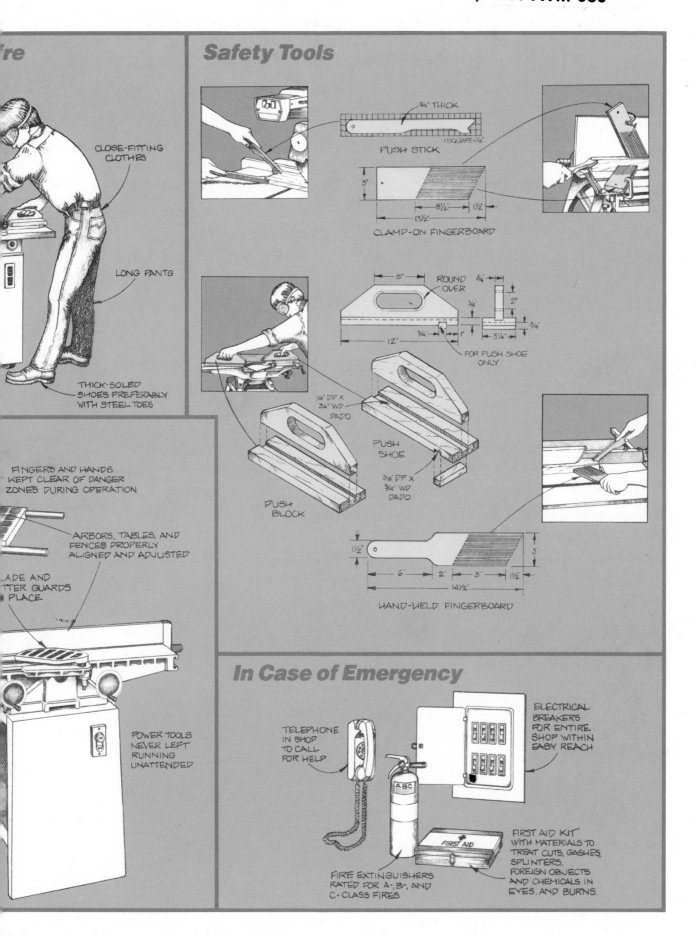

Safety Tools

CLOSE-FITTING CLOTHES

LONG PANTS

THICK-SOLED SHOES PREFERABLY WITH STEEL TOES

3/4" THICK

PUSH STICK

1 SQUARE = 1/2"

CLAMP-ON FINGERBOARD

3"

8 1/2" 1 1/2"

13 1/2"

ROUND OVER

5"

3/4"

3/4"

2"

12"

3/4" 1"

3 1/4"

3/4"

FOR PUSH SHOE ONLY

1/4" DP X 3/4" WD DADO

PUSH SHOE

3/8" DP X 3/4" WD DADO

PUSH BLOCK

FINGERS AND HANDS KEPT CLEAR OF DANGER ZONES DURING OPERATION

ARBORS, TABLES, AND FENCES PROPERLY ALIGNED AND ADJUSTED

BLADE AND CUTTER GUARDS IN PLACE

POWER TOOLS NEVER LEFT RUNNING UNATTENDED

1 1/2"

3"

6" 2" 5" 1 1/2"

14 1/2"

HAND-HELD FINGERBOARD

In Case of Emergency

TELEPHONE IN SHOP TO CALL FOR HELP

ELECTRICAL BREAKERS FOR ENTIRE SHOP WITHIN EASY REACH

ABC

FIRST AID

FIRE EXTINGUISHERS RATED FOR A-, B-, AND C- CLASS FIRES

FIRST AID KIT WITH MATERIALS TO TREAT CUTS, GASHES, SPLINTERS, FOREIGN OBJECTS AND CHEMICALS IN EYES, AND BURNS.

·BUILD·IT·BETTER·YOURSELF·
WOODWORKING PROJECTS

Accents for the Country Home

Collected and Written
by Nick Engler

Rodale Press
Emmaus, Pennsylvania

Series Editor: William H. Hylton
Managing Editor/Author: Nick Engler
Editor: Roger Yepsen
Copy Editor: Mary Green
Graphic Designer: Linda Watts
Draftspersons: Mary Jane Favorite
              Chris Walendzak
Photography: Karen Callahan
Cover Photography: Mitch Mandel
Cover Photograph Stylist: Janet C. Vera
Proofreader: Hue Park
Typesetting by Computer Typography, Huber Heights, Ohio
Interior Illustrations by O'Neil & Associates, Dayton, Ohio
Endpaper Illustrations by Mary Jane Favorite
Produced by Bookworks, Inc., West Milton, Ohio

If you have any questions or comments concerning this book, please write:
    Rodale Press
    Book Reader Service
    33 East Minor Street
    Emmaus, PA 18098

Library of Congress Cataloging-in-Publication Data

Engler, Nick.
    Accents for the country home/collected and written by Nick
    Engler.
        p.   cm.—(Build-it-better-yourself woodworking
        projects)
    ISBN 0–87857–841–2 hardcover
    ISBN 0–87857–842–0 paperback
    1. Woodwork.   2. House furnishings.   I. Title.   II. Series:
Engler, Nick. Build-it-better-yourself woodworking projects.
TT180.E615   1989
684'.08—dc20
                                                      90–8324
                                                      CIP

Distributed in the book trade by St. Martin's Press

2 4 6 8 10 9 7 5 3   hardcover
2 4 6 8 10 9 7 5 3 1 paperback

Contents

Chust for So

Folklorists often argue over the true meaning of the colorful hex signs that adorn the barns of southeastern Pennsylvania. Some say these are magical charms, painted by a superstitious people to bring good fortune. Others contend they are purely for decoration. If you ask a Pennsylvania Dutch farmer why he paints hex signs on his barn, he is liable to imitate the stereotyped accent of his Germanic forefathers and say with a sly smile: "Chust for so."

So it is with many of the small country artifacts in this book. They may have once served a purpose, but their original use has changed or been forgotten over the years. Still, we admire their beauty and ingenuity, and keep making them "chust for so."

A Few Necessary Skills

These projects are drawn from every area of early American country life, representing a range of designs. As you look over the instructions, however, you may be struck by some similarities in the skills needed to make them. There are many complex patterns to be cut — more than in ordinary woodworking projects. Often, the projects are partially carved. They aren't finely sculpted, necessarily, but numerous parts must be shaped three-dimensionally. Finally, a majority of the projects are painted rather than finished. Some of this painting is quite detailed.

Enlarging patterns is a tedious chore. Carving and painting can be equally time-consuming, particularly if you have limited experience with either craft. To help your woodworking projects progress quickly and easily, here are some tips on these three areas.

Enlarging and Transferring Patterns

Whenever possible, the patterns are printed full size. A caption under the pattern will say, "Printed at 100%." These don't have to be enlarged, of course. Just make a photocopy of them.

In many cases, the captions will tell you the patterns are printed at 77 percent, 60 percent, or 46 percent of full size. These reductions were calculated so you can enlarge the patterns with a photocopier. *Some* photocopiers can enlarge and reduce documents. You can usually find these at quick-print shops and copying businesses. Look in the Yellow Pages of your phone directory under "Photo Copying" and "Copying and Duplicating Service."

Enlarging/reducing copiers all have several standard settings, one of which is a "Letter-to-Legal-Size" enlargement. At this setting, the machine will enlarge the patterns *approximately* 129 percent. (The actual percentage varies slightly depending on the make of the copier.) Enlarge the 77 percent patterns once to bring them up to full size. For the 60 percent patterns, enlarge them once, then enlarge the copies. If the patterns are printed at 46 percent, take this a step further, enlarging the pattern *three* times. (See Figure 1.) Here's the math, showing how to arrive at a full-size (100% or 1.00) pattern:

$$0.77 \times 1.29 = 1.00$$
$$0.60 \times 1.29 \times 1.29 = 1.00$$
$$0.46 \times 1.29 \times 1.29 \times 1.29 = 1.00$$

1/When you enlarge a pattern more than once, turn it 90° each time you copy it. This will minimize distortion.

Note: Although photocopying is much easier than traditional enlarging methods, *it is not accurate*. The lens may distort the image, or the copier may be improperly adjusted. If so, the enlarged pattern will be slightly larger or smaller than full size, or expanded in one direction more than another. These discrepancies shouldn't matter for most of the patterns in this book; the shapes and the dimensions aren't critical. So long as they're close to full size, the projects will turn out just fine.

Some patterns are too big to enlarge on a photocopier. In this case, there will be no percentage printed under the pattern. Use a pantograph, an overhead projector, or the squares method to enlarge these patterns.

Once you have enlarged the pattern, there are several simple ways to transfer it to the stock. If you want to save the enlarged pattern, tape a piece of carbon paper on the wood, and tape the pattern on top of that. Trace the lines of the pattern with a used-up ball-point pen. When you've finished, remove the pattern and the carbon paper.

If the pattern is expendable, spray a light coat of adhesive on the back and stick it on the wood. Cut both the wood and the pattern, then peel the pattern off. If any adhesive remains on the wood, wipe it off with acetone.

Carving

The first step in successfully carving a piece is choosing a proper wood. It must be durable, easy to cut, and provide what experienced carvers call "control." Wood has good control if it doesn't chip, break, flake, or split as you carve. You can cut away a small amount of stock without accidentally removing too much.

Three species of wood have all these qualities — basswood, butternut, and lauan mahogany. Of the three, most carvers favor basswood. It's relatively strong and easy to work, and has excellent control. It's also fairly easy to find — you can purchase it through many mail-order woodworking suppliers and at most lumberyards that sell hardwoods.

The second step is to use the right tools. Woodworkers often purchase sets of so-called "carving chisels" and expect to use them for occasional carving tasks. These are actually *detail* chisels, more useful for cleaning up joinery than for carving. Instead, you can carve most three-dimensional shapes with a single *bench knife* (or *carving knife*) — a 5"- to 6"-long wooden handle with a short, straight blade. To make carving tasks a little easier, it's helpful to have a variety of curved and straight blades. Look for a carving knife set with a single handle and several interchangeable blades. (See Figure 2.)

As you carve, you'll find that you can pare away most of the waste with two basic techniques. In the first, you use your thumb as an anchor. Grasp the knife in one hand and hook the thumb of that hand over the end of the stock. Squeeze your thumb and fingers together as if you were tightening your grip on something. This will draw the knife toward you, shaving the stock. (See Figure 3.)

In the second technique, you use your thumb as a pivot. Grasp the stock in one hand and the knife in the other. Rest the back of the blade against the thumb of the stock hand, with the cutting edge facing away from you. Use the handle like a lever, pulling it toward you. This will force the blade to cut away from you. (See Figure 4.)

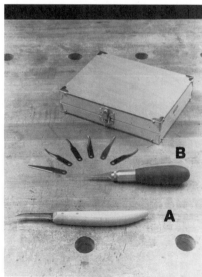

*2/*To make basic carvings, you need a **bench knife** (A). A **carving knife set** (B) with several interchangeable blades is also useful.

*3/*When using your thumb as an anchor, keep it below or to one side of the surface that you're carving. If the knife slips as you pull it toward you, you won't accidentally cut your thumb.

Both of these techniques remove small amounts of wood with each stroke. This reduces the chance that you'll remove too much, and requires minimal effort. You'll be able to carve longer and more comfortably without tiring.

Painting

Like carving, painting a detailed piece depends on choosing the proper materials. The wood should be light colored, as white as possible. Basswood, maple, and white pine are all good choices. You can also use birch and poplar, if you avoid the darker heartwood sections. A dark wood may show through the paint — especially lighter tones — and dull the color.

Choose paint that covers well and spreads easily. You also want a wide selection of colors to choose from, and these should remain bright without fading over time. Finally, the paint must dry quickly and thoroughly so you can apply other finishes over it. Two types of paint have all of these qualities — latex and acrylics. Latex is usually available only in quantities of a pint or more. Because of this, it's best used when you have a lot of surface area to paint. Acrylics are available in much smaller quantities. (See Figure 5.)

Before you paint, sand the surface and wipe it with a tack cloth to remove any dust. Don't prime the surface. When you paint details, primer may actually prevent the paint from covering or spreading properly.

If you can, start painting with the lighter colors and work your way to the darker tones. It's much more time consuming to put light colors over dark. Lighter colors are less opaque, and you must apply several coats so the dark ones won't show through.

Colors can be shaded or blended in several ways. First, you can dilute a darker color with water to make it very thin, then apply it over a lighter color. (This is called a *wash*.) Soften the darker color even more by rubbing the thin, wet paint with your finger. The lighter color will show through, making the darker one look like a shadow.

You can also "dry brush" one color over another. Dip a clean, *dry* brush in a color, then wipe most of it off on a piece of paper or scrap wood. Lightly paint the surface with the lightly loaded brush. The dry-brushed paint will go on very thinly, allowing the color underneath to show through only slightly changed.

Finally, you can blend the boundary between two colors on a surface, while the paint is still wet. This works best when the two areas are close in color. Work quickly, overlapping the lighter color with a thin layer of the darker color. Wet your brush in clean water, then blend the boundary area.

To protect the colors from dirt and wear, apply a coat of clear shellac, lacquer, varnish, or polyurethane over them. Make sure the paint is completely dry; otherwise, the clear finishes may cloud. If you want the paint to look old, tint the finish with a little burnt umber artist's oil paint. (You can buy this in the same stores that sell acrylics.) The burnt umber gives the finish a warm reddish-brown cast that dulls the colors, making them look worn and faded.

4/When using your thumb as a pivot, you can easily control the amount of stock you cut. Simply adjust the contact point between your thumb and the knife blade. The further this point is from the knife tip, the more stock you will cut.

5/You can buy acrylics in tubes or small plastic squeeze bottles. If you purchase tubes, you may have to mix colors to get a range of tones and shades. Bottled acrylics come already mixed in more than one hundred colors. You can mix them further to create still more. Both tubes and bottles are available at arts-and-crafts stores, as well as many paint suppliers.

Miniature Rocking Horse

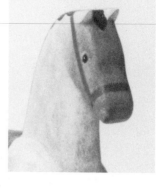

Miniature rocking horses have delighted children since ancient times, long before the appearance of rocking horses that were large enough to ride. Archaeologists have found miniatures in Egyptian and Persian tombs. The first known examples of rideable rocking horses date to medieval times. These were used to train young boys destined to become knights.

The appearance of the larger rocking horses did little to discourage the popularity of miniatures. They were manufactured in great numbers in Europe and imported to America during most of the nineteenth century. Some came with wooden dolls — usually cavalry soldiers — to sit in the miniature saddles. These imported toys apparently were the prized possessions of many well-to-do American youngsters; folk portraits of children from the 1800s often show them with a miniature rocking horse.

Parents who couldn't afford the imports sometimes made them for their children. The horse shown is typical of many handmade American miniatures. The parts are simple cutouts, glued and pegged together. The horse is rounded and rough-carved to give it some shape. The tail and the mane are scraps of yarn, glued to the wood. ●

Materials List

FINISHED DIMENSIONS

PARTS

A.	Body	¾" x 3½" x 5½"
B.	Flanks (2)	½" x 3⅞" x 6½"
C.	Runners (2)	¼" x 2½" x 9¼"
D.	Spacers (5)	⅜" x ½" x 2"
E.	Wedge	⅛" x ⅛" x ⅜"

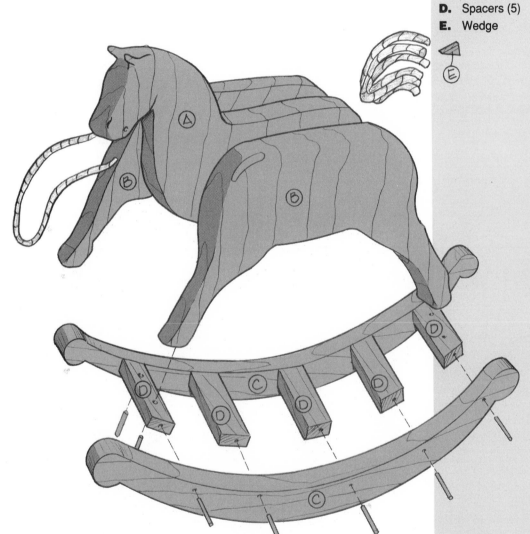

EXPLODED VIEW

HARDWARE

Round toothpicks (10–14)
Brown or black yarn (5"–10")
Black string (4"–5")

1
Select the stock and cut the parts to size. Since you'll be painting the rocking horse, you should make the parts from a durable, light-colored wood. This wood should also be easy to carve, if you want to sculpt the features. Basswood is the best choice, followed by butternut and lauan mahogany. (For more information on choosing woods for carving, see the introductory chapter, Chust for So.)

After you choose the stock, plane it to the thicknesses needed — ¾" for the body, ½" for the flanks and spacers, and ¼" for the runners. Cut the parts to size.

2
Cut the shapes. Enlarge the *Body Pattern, Flank Pattern,* and *Runner Pattern.* Trace the patterns on the stock, then cut them out with a band saw or scroll saw. Sand the sawed edges.

TRY THIS! To save time, stack the flank pieces and tape them together. Trace the pattern on the top piece only, then cut both pieces at once.

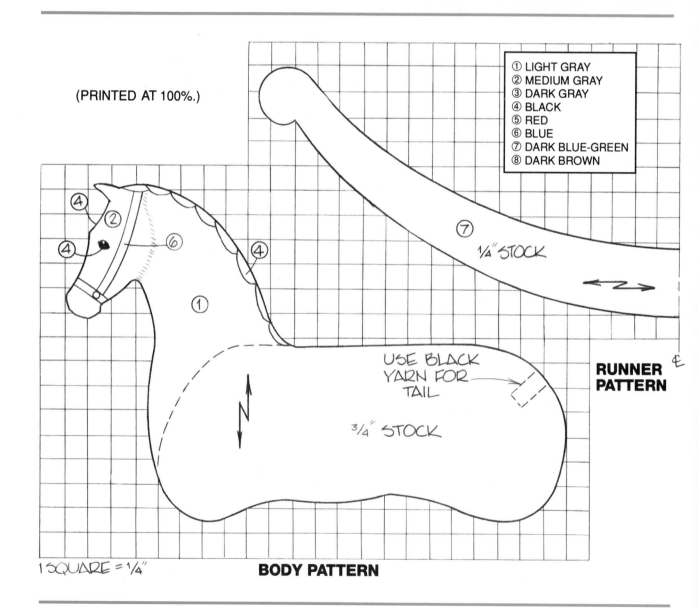

(PRINTED AT 100%.)

① LIGHT GRAY
② MEDIUM GRAY
③ DARK GRAY
④ BLACK
⑤ RED
⑥ BLUE
⑦ DARK BLUE-GREEN
⑧ DARK BROWN

¼" STOCK

RUNNER PATTERN

USE BLACK YARN FOR TAIL

¾" STOCK

1 SQUARE = ¼"

BODY PATTERN

3

Carve the flank and body parts. If you want to sculpt the parts of the horse, you'll find it's easier to carve most of the features *before* you glue the flank and body parts together. You don't have to be an experienced carver to create a realistic horse. This project is very simple to carve:

■ Round over the *outside* edges of the chest, torso, and withers on the flank parts. Remember, these parts should be mirror images of each other.

■ Round *both* the inside and outside edges of the legs, ankles, and hooves, also on the flank parts. (See Figure 1.)

■ Round all edges of the neck, head, and nose on the body part.

■ Remove stock between the ears to define them. The ears are also on the body part. (See Figure 2.)

1/The horse does not require intricate carving. To create most of the features, all you need to do is round the edges.

2/The only features that aren't created by rounding over the edges are the ears. To make these, simply remove some of the stock between them.

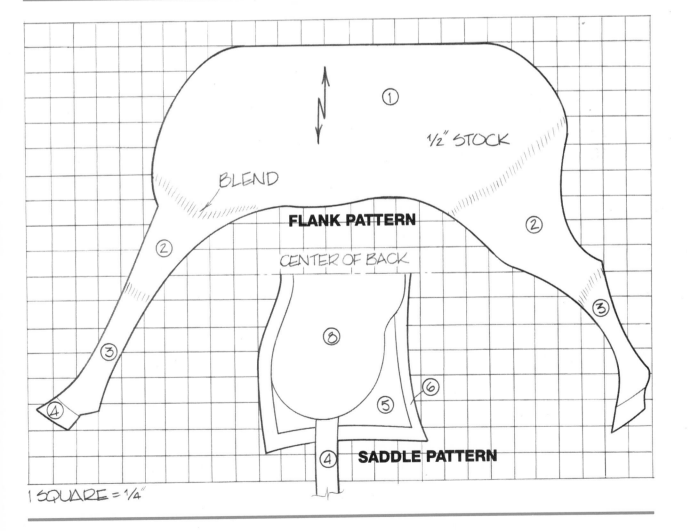

① ½" STOCK

BLEND

FLANK PATTERN

② ②

CENTER OF BACK

③ ③

② ③

⑧

⑥

⑤

④

④ **SADDLE PATTERN**

1 SQUARE = ¼"

4 Glue the horse together.

When you've finished carving, glue the parts of the horse together — flanks on the outside, body in the middle. When the glue dries, sand all the joints clean and flush.

Drill a ¼"-diameter, ⅜"-deep hole in the rump to mount the tail, and a ⅛"-diameter hole through the nose for the bridle. Finish sand the horse, smoothing the features and removing any chisel marks.

5 Assemble the rocker.

Finish sand the runners and spacers. Glue the parts together, tacking them with wire brads until the glue has dried. Before the glue sets up, check that all four of the horse's feet will rest solidly on the front and back spacers. If they won't, move one or both of the spacers.

When the glue dries, remove the brads one by one. Replace each brad in turn with a wooden peg made from a round toothpick. After you remove a brad, drill a ¹⁄₁₆"-diameter, ½"-deep hole through the runner and into the end of the spacer. Trim ¼" – ⅜" off the point of a toothpick. Dip the toothpick in glue, and press it into the hole. It should wedge itself tight; if it doesn't, trim a little more off the narrow end. Let the glue dry, then cut the toothpick off and sand it flush with the runner. (See Figure 3.)

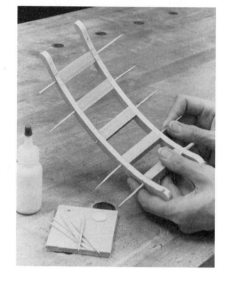

3/Peg the rocker assembly together with round toothpicks. You can trim them easily with a wire cutter.

6 Paint the horse and rocker assemblies.

Just as it was easier to carve the horse parts before you assembled them, it will be easier to paint the horse and rocker assemblies before you fasten them together. Apply latex or acrylic paint, following the color codes.

Note: The horse shown is a dapple-gray. If you would rather paint it another color, get some picture books on horses from your local library. Use these as guides while you paint.

7 Assemble the horse and rocker.

Attach the horse to the front and back spacers with epoxy glue. Let the glue set, then drill ¹⁄₁₆"-diameter, ½"-deep holes up through the spacers and into the hooves. Peg the horse assembly to the rocker assembly with round toothpicks, in the same manner that you pegged the rocker assembly together. Trim the toothpicks and sand them flush with the spacers. Touch up any paint that needs it.

8 Glue the tail in the horse.

Cut several pieces of yarn, 2½" – 3" long. (The number of yarn pieces you need depends on how thick the yarn is.) Make a small wooden wedge, about ⅛" x ⅛" x ⅜". Put a little glue in the hole in the horse's rump. Bend the lengths of yarn in two, and stuff the bent portions into the hole. Dip the wedge in glue, then press it into the hole to secure the yarn. After the glue dries, trim the tail so all the pieces of yarn are the same length. Thread the bridle string through the nose and join the ends with a square knot.

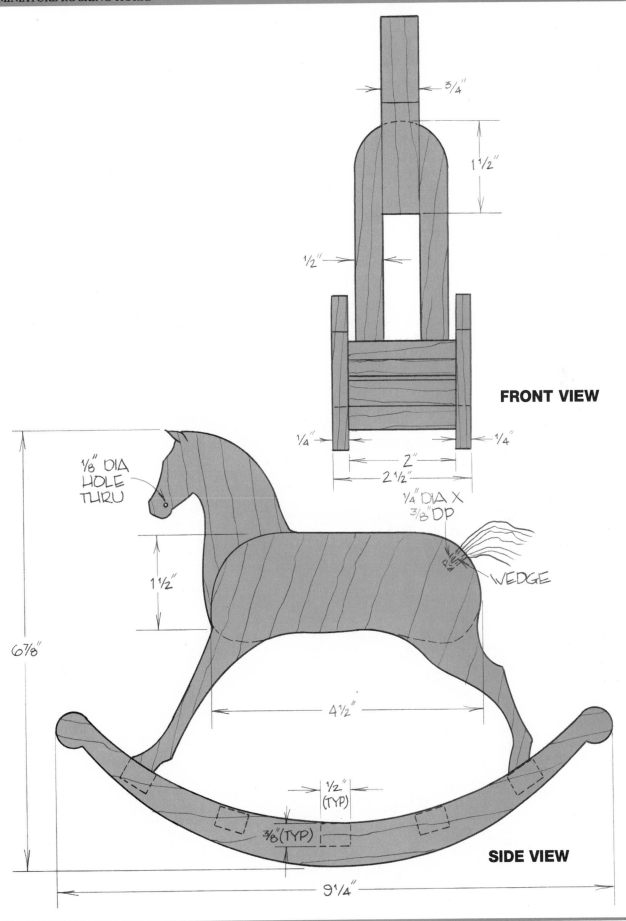

FRONT VIEW

¾"

1½"

½"

¼" DIA X
⅜" DP

WEDGE

¼"

¼"

2"

2 ½"

⅛" DIA
HOLE
THRU

1½"

6⅞"

4½"

½"
(TYP)

⅜" (TYP)

SIDE VIEW

9¼"

Adjustable Candlestand

As a candle burns, the light from the flame strikes the objects around it from an increasingly lower angle. If you are studying or writing by candlelight, you must either raise the candle or adjust your work to keep it properly illuminated.

The eighteenth- and nineteenth-century people who depended on candles for light at night found it was easier to elevate the candle periodically than it was to move the work continually. They invented several different mechanisms to do this. The candlestand shown is perhaps the most effective and the simplest to operate. Two candle holders are mounted on an arm, and the arm is mounted on a threaded post. Each time the arm makes a counterclockwise revolution around the post, it elevates the candle holders about ⅛".

Like most country pieces, this is a simple, straightforward project to make. Most of the pieces are shaped on the lathe; the arm is cut on a band saw. However, the project does require a special tool — you *must* have a 1"-diameter wood threader and tap to cut the threads in the post and arm. Most woodworking mail-order supply houses sell hand-operated wood threaders (sometimes called thread boxes or box threaders). If you prefer power-operated tools, you can obtain a wood-threading attachment for routers from:

Beall Tool Company
541 Swans Road NE
Newark, OH 43055

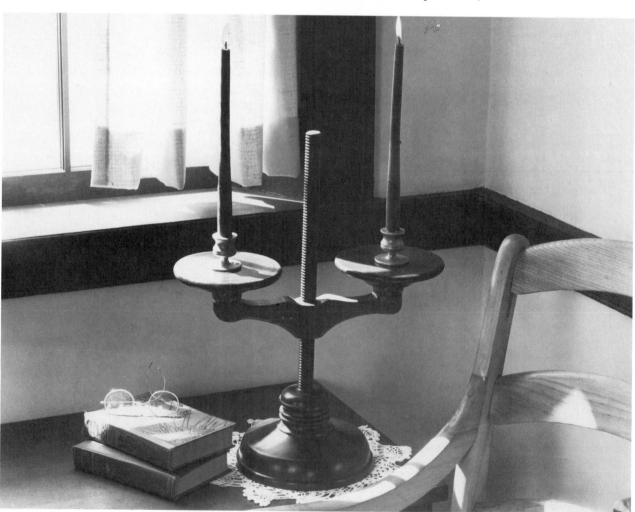

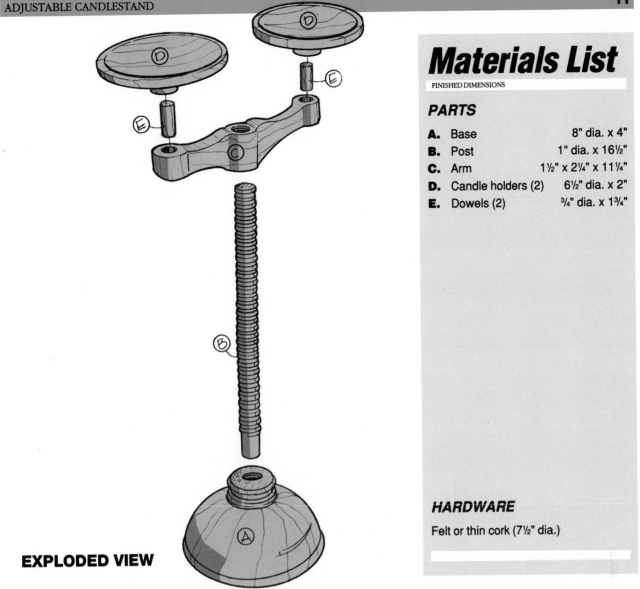

EXPLODED VIEW

Materials List

FINISHED DIMENSIONS

PARTS

A.	Base	8" dia. x 4"
B.	Post	1" dia. x 16½"
C.	Arm	1½" x 2¼" x 11¼"
D.	Candle holders (2)	6½" dia. x 2"
E.	Dowels (2)	¾" dia. x 1¾"

HARDWARE

Felt or thin cork (7½" dia.)

---

1 Select and prepare the stock.
Candlestands were made from many different types of hardwood. You want to choose a wood species into which you can easily cut screw threads, and yet it should stand up to constant use. The traditional choices for threaded projects are yellow birch, hard maple, and hickory — in that order. Close-grained hardwoods such as cherry and apple also work well. So do some of the medium-hard open-grained woods like walnut (used in the candlestand shown) and Philippine mahogany. Avoid open-grained woods that splinter easily (oak and ash); tough, fibrous woods that are difficult to cut across the grain (poplar and elm); and woods that are too soft to be durable (lauan mahogany, cedar, and sugar pine).

When you have chosen the stock, cut or glue the turning blocks you need to make the base, post, and candle holders. Remember that the grain direction of a turning block should parallel the axis of rotation. You may be tempted to make blocks for the base and holders with the grain perpendicular to rotation — this seems easier and more economical. But these blocks are extremely hard to turn because the chisel wants to catch the grain and dig in.

Warning: When making turning blocks, always glue the wood long grain to long grain; avoid end-grain joints. Make sure that all glue seams are tight and uniform — there must be no gaps. Let the glue cure for *at least* 24 hours before turning the block. *This is extremely important!* Woodworking glues do not reach their full strength until they have set for a day, even though some set up in less than an hour. If you turn a block before the glue is completely cured, it may come apart on the lathe.

2 **Turn the base and holders.** The base and the candle holders are *faceplate* turnings. To shape them, you must screw the stock to a metal disk or plate, which in turn is mounted on the drive shaft of the lathe.

It's best not to mount the turning blocks directly on the faceplate. This may interfere with your work — the chisel could catch on the metal disk. And when you remove the work from the plate, you will have to fill the screw holes. Instead, glue the turning block to a wooden *mounting block* and screw the mounting block to the faceplate. This mounting block should be ¾"–1" thick (as thick as the screws are long), and the same diameter (or slightly smaller) than the diameter of your turning. Put a piece of paper between the mounting block and the turning block as you glue them up. (See Figure 1.) After you finish the turning, this paper will make it easier to separate the two blocks.

1/To make it easier to separate the turning block and the mounting block, put a piece of paper between them when you glue them together. Use a **single** sheet of newspaper or typing paper — multiple sheets, thick paper, and poster board will not work. Put a generous amount of glue on **both** sides of the paper, and clamp the blocks together.

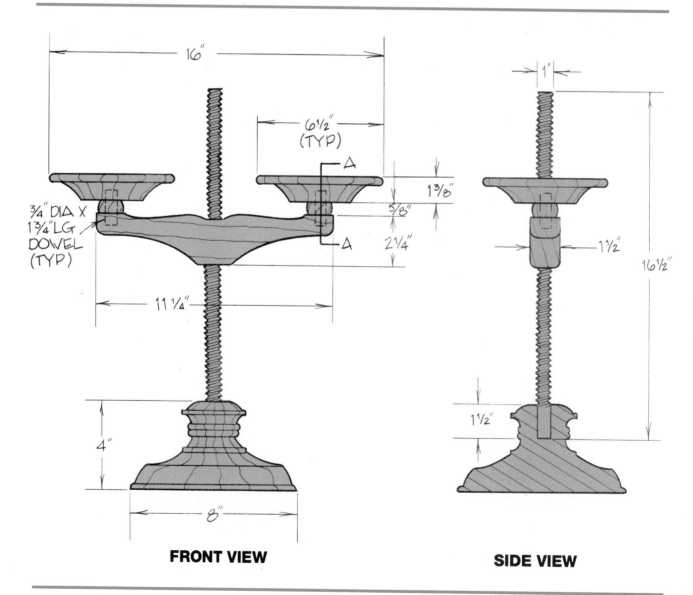

¾" DIA X 1¾" LG DOWEL (TYP)

16"

6½" (TYP)

11 ¼"

4"

8"

FRONT VIEW

1"

1⅜"

⅝"

2¼"

1½"

1½"

16½"

SIDE VIEW

Warning: When you glue turning blocks to mounting blocks, the 24-hour rule applies: Let the glue cure for *at least* one full day before turning the wood.

After the glue dries, mount one of the holder blocks on the lathe, and turn the shape shown in the *Candle Holder Pattern*. (See Figure 2.) Form the holder on the lathe with the bottom facing *away* from the mounting block. Finish sand the shape, then mark the location of the mounting hole on the bottom.

> **TRY THIS!** To find the exact center of a faceplate turning, run the lathe and look at the stock. The center is the one spot on the wood that appears to be stationary.

Many lathes allow you to drill holes in faceplate turnings. If you have this equipment, drill the mounting hole now. Mount a chuck on the lathe tailstock, and clamp a ¾"-diameter bit in the chuck. Run the lathe at a low speed and advance the bit (or the turning) until the mounting hole is 1" deep. (See Figure 3.) If you don't have this equipment, make the hole on a drill press after you remove the stock from the lathe.

To separate the candle holder and the mounting block, place a chisel on the glue seam and tap the chisel sharply with a mallet. (See Figure 4.) Rotate the turning 20°–30° and repeat. The fiber of the paper will eventually give way, and the two pieces of wood will part cleanly.

Run the lathe to find the center of the mounting block, then drill a ¾"-diameter hole partway through the center. Glue the holder and the mounting block back together with the *bottom* of the holder against the mounting block. Use a short length of ¾" dowel to center the turning block on the mounting block, but *do not* glue the dowel in either block. Once again, put paper between the two pieces of wood. Cut a ¾"-diameter hole in the paper so it fits over the dowel.

2/Turn the shape on the candle holder at a low to medium speed. Since you're cutting end grain primarily, it's easier to make scraping cuts. Hold the chisel at nearly 90° to the work and feed it firmly into the wood. If you hold the chisel at a smaller angle (as you do when shearing), it may dig into the grain.

3/If your lathe is equipped with a chuck, use it to drill the mounting hole in the candle holders. Remember that you're drilling end grain — feed the bit (or the work) slowly so it doesn't burn.

4/Use a chisel as a wedge to pry the turning block from the mounting block. Since the paper between the blocks is weaker than the wood, the blocks will come apart without damaging the turning.

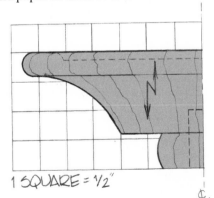

1 SQUARE = ½"

CANDLE HOLDER PATTERN
(PRINTED AT 60%. ENLARGE
2 TIMES ON PHOTOCOPIER AT 129%.)

TRY THIS! When you clamp the two blocks together, a little glue inevitably squeezes into the ¾"-diameter holes. This will cause the dowel to stick, and make it difficult to separate the blocks. To prevent the problem, wax the dowel.

After the glue cures completely, turn the lip and the hollow in the top of the holder, as shown in *Section A.* (See Figure 5.) Feed the chisel very gently, particularly when working near the edge of the turning. The glue joint that holds the blocks together is small — much smaller than it was when you made the first portion of the turning. If you press too hard with the chisel, the joint may break. When you complete the holder, finish sand the lip and the hollow. Then separate the turning from the mounting block in the same manner that you did before.

Repeat this procedure for the second holder. Then turn the base in a similar manner, cutting the shape shown in the *Base Pattern.* Drill a 1"-diameter hole in the base for the post. Sand the bottoms of the base and the holders with a belt sander to remove any glue or paper that remains.

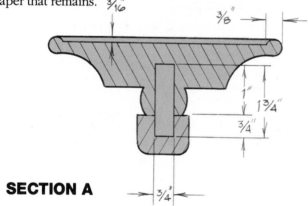

SECTION A

5/To turn the lip and the hollow in the holder, flip it top-for-bottom and glue it back to the mounting block. Carefully center the holder on the block so the hollow will be centered in the holder.

Note: None of the turning patterns is critical; there's no need to make up a template or guide and follow it exactly. You can make up your own patterns if you wish, so long as you follow the general dimensions in the Materials List.

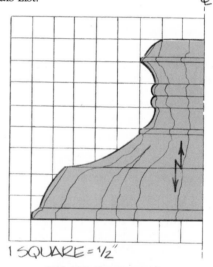

1 SQUARE = ½"

BASE PATTERN
(PRINTED AT 46%. ENLARGE
3 TIMES ON PHOTOCOPIER AT 129%.)

3 **Turn the post.** If you're making this project from common domestic hardwoods such as walnut, cherry, birch, or maple, you may be able to buy 1"-diameter dowels from nearby hardwood dealers or mail-order woodworking suppliers. If not, you must spindle-turn the dowel stock needed for the post. Use a steadyrest to keep the long, slender turning from whipping on the lathe.

Only the bottom 1½" (the portion that mounts in the base) needs to be exactly 1" in diameter. The remainder can be 1" or slightly smaller — but no smaller than $^{15}/_{16}$". As you work, check the diameter often with calipers. When you finish, *don't* cut the stock to length. Leave

both ends intact until *after* you've cut the threads. Later on, you'll need to mount the threaded post back on the lathe.

TRY THIS! There is a chance that the next step — threading the post — will chew up the stock. Sometimes hidden flaws in the wood don't become apparent until you start cutting the threads. You may want to have two or three lengths of post stock, just in case.

4 **Cut the threads in the post.** You must apply linseed oil to the post before you cut the threads — the oil lubricates the threading cutter and keeps the stock from chipping as you cut. Put several layers of masking tape over the bottom 1½" of the post to protect this end from linseed oil. Otherwise, you won't be able to glue the post into the base. Wipe the post liberally with linseed oil and let it soak in for several minutes. Then wipe the post with oil a second time.

If you're using a wood threader, clamp the stock in a vise, top end up. Put the threader over the top end, and slowly turn it clockwise around the post. Press down gently until you feel the cutter bite into the wood. After a few revolutions, the threader will feed itself and you shouldn't have to press down. Continue to turn the threader slowly until you have cut the male threads you need. (See Figure 6.) To remove the tool from the post, reverse the direction of rotation, turning counterclockwise.

If you're using a router attachment, there are two significant changes in this procedure. First, carefully set up and adjust the tool according to the manufacturer's instructions. Second, feed the dowel into the tool, instead of running the tool along the dowel.

After you cut the threads, mount the post back on the lathe. Run the lathe at low speed and lightly sand the threaded portion. (See Figure 7.) Sanding is very important if you want the threads to remain in good condition, because the threader leaves behind a pointed crest on the thread. This point chips easily, since the grain runs nearly perpendicular to the thread, and sanding removes it.

6/The trick to cutting clean threads with a box threader is to use plenty of linseed oil for lubrication and to keep the threader turning slowly and **steadily.** If the threads chip, try turning the threader a little faster or a little slower. If that doesn't work, try another piece of dowel stock.

7/To keep the threads from chipping, very lightly sand the threaded portion of the post with the lathe at a low speed. If you spin the post too fast or press too hard, the threads may chip anyway.

5 **Cut the threads in the arm.** Cut the arm stock to size. Enlarge the *Arm Patterns* and trace them on the stock. Be careful that both the top and the side patterns line up properly. Drill the holes shown on the *Arm Pattern/Top View* — a ⅞"-diameter hole through the middle of the arm, and two mounting holes, ¾" in diameter and ¾" deep, at either end.

Cut female threads in the middle hole, so the arm can be mounted on the post. Make these threads as you did the male threads, but using a tap instead of the wood threader or routing attachment. Apply linseed oil to the walls of the hole to lubricate the tap, and clamp the stock in a vise. Place the tap in the hole and turn it clockwise, pressing down gently. As the tap bites into the wood, it will feed itself. (See Figure 8.) Keep it turning slowly and steadily until it exits the bottom of the arm stock.

8/Cut the female threads in the arm stock with a tap. This will require a good deal more effort than cutting the male threads. You can use a long bar or a pipe for additional leverage if needed to keep the tap turning steadily.

6

Saw the shape of the arm. To shape the arm, make a compound cut on the band saw. Saw the top shape first, saving the scrap. Tape the scrap back to the arm stock, turn the stock on its side, and cut the side pattern. Remove the tape and the scrap, then sand the arm to remove the saw marks.

7

Assemble and finish the candlestand. Cut two 1¾" lengths of ¾"-diameter dowels. Glue the dowels in either end of the arm, then glue the candle holders to the dowels and the arm. Remove the tape from the bottom of the post, and glue it in the 1"-diameter hole in the base.

Wipe the threaded parts with mineral spirits to remove the linseed oil, and do any necessary touch-up sanding. Apply a penetrating finish to the arm and base assemblies. Use something that soaks into the wood, such as tung oil or Danish oil. Finishes that build up on the surface, such as varnish, may cause the arm to bind on the post.

When the finish dries, glue a felt or cork pad to the bottom surface of the base. Wax and buff the assemblies (taking care not to wax the pad), and screw the arm onto the post.

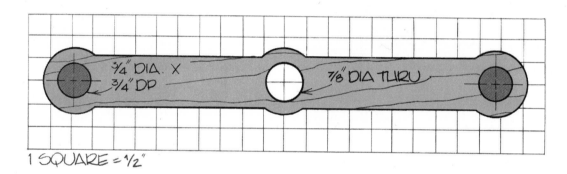

¾" DIA. X ¾" DP   ⅞" DIA THRU

1 SQUARE = ½"

ARM PATTERN/TOP VIEW

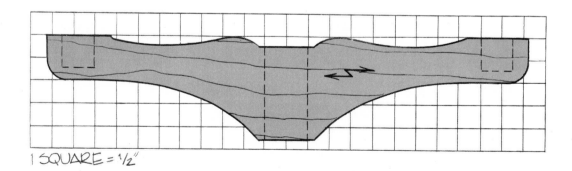

1 SQUARE = ½"

ARM PATTERN/SIDE VIEW

(PRINTED AT 46%. ENLARGE 3 TIMES ON PHOTOCOPIER AT 129%.)

Barn Signs

Country folks often hung hand-painted signs on their barns and out-buildings. Some were advertisements, announcing a farmer's specialty to passersby. Others were blessings, asking for protection and good fortune for the farm and family. Still others were charms, meant to ward off lightning strikes, disease, and other disasters. All these signs were colorful and decorative, adding a bit of fancy to otherwise plain and utilitarian buildings.

The barn signs shown represent the two best-known types — animal signs and hex signs. Livestock and dairy farmers used animal signs to advertise the type and breed of animal that they raised. These signs were usually simple cutouts, shaped and painted to look like horses, cows, bulls, pigs, sheep, goats, geese, chickens, dogs — any farm or sporting animal. This rustic silhouette of a cow might have hung on a dairy barn, telling anyone who might be interested that the resident dairyman milked a herd of holstein cattle.

Intricate, brightly colored hex signs have adorned the barns of some Pennsylvania Dutch for about 150 years. The origin of

these signs is surrounded by controversy. Some folklorists claim they were purely decorative; others say they were superstitious charms. According to the latter view, certain symbols, when placed within a circle, could avert bad fortune or encourage good. Some of these symbols were preventive. They barred witches from entering the barn, neutralized curses, kept livestock from getting sick, and so on. Others were affirmative. They petitioned for good weather, romance, a sound marriage, abundance, fertility, good health, success, strength of mind and character, and dozens of other desirable things, both physical and spiritual. The sign shown supposedly promotes abundance, faith, love, and goodwill toward your fellowman.

Materials List

FINISHED DIMENSIONS

PARTS

A. Cow (small)   ½" x 9¾" x 14⅞"
     (large)   ½" x 19½" x 29¾"

B. Sheep (small)   ½" x 8⅜" x 8¾"
     (large)   ½" x 16¾" x 17½"

C. Pig (small)   ½" x 6" x 10"
     (large)   ½" x 12" x 20"

D. Goat (small)   ½" x 6½" x 9⅜"
     (large)   ½" x 13" x 18¾"

E. Hex sign   (variable) dia.* x ½"

F. Brackets
     (2 per sign)**   ¾" x 1" x (variable)

G. Stop blocks
     (2 per sign)**   ¾" x 1" x 3"

*Hex signs can be any size — the one shown is 16" across. However, they **must** be round.*

**Needed for an outdoor sign only.*

HARDWARE

For an indoor sign:

¼" Eye screws (2)
Picture-hanging wire (length variable)
Picture hook (size variable)

For an outdoor sign:

#10 x 1" Flathead wood screws (6–8)
#10 x 2" Flathead wood screws (4–6)
2" L-hooks (2–3)

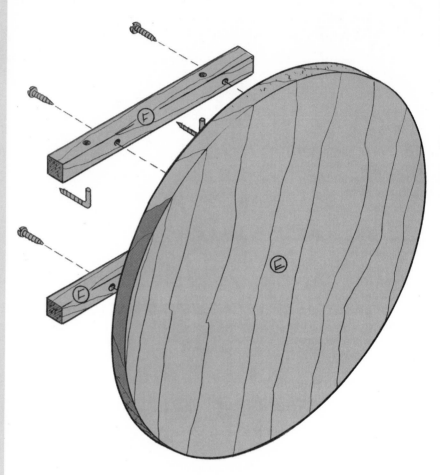

EXPLODED VIEW

1 Select and prepare the stock.

Before purchasing the lumber for this project, decide whether you want a sign that looks old and weathered or one that looks bright and new. Also decide where you want to display the sign — inside or out.

Use solid lumber if you either want the sign to look old or plan to hang it indoors. Most old-time barn signs were painted on solid wood and then hung outdoors. Over the years, the wood shrunk and cracked. You can duplicate this effect by using old barn wood to make your sign.

If you can't get old barn wood, use new softwood lumber, preferably white pine or redwood. After you cut the shape of the sign, take it to a sandblasting service. Have them *lightly* blast the surface of the wood with fine sand or tiny glass beads. As the sand strikes the surface, it wears away the soft summer growth (light-colored wood) faster than the harder winter growth (darker annual rings). The surface becomes uneven, making the wood look old and weathered.

If you want the sign to look new or plan to hang it outdoors, use commercial signboard or MDO-board. (MDO stand for *medium density overlay*.) This outdoor plywood is covered on one side with paper to provide a smooth, even painting surface. The paper also protects the wood from the weather, if it's properly treated and finished. MDO-board comes in 2' x 4', 4' x 4', and 4' x 8' sheets. It's available from most commercial lumberyards, although it may be a special-order item.

2 ***Cut the shape of the sign.*** If you're making an animal sign, enlarge one of the patterns shown. For a large outdoor sign, let each square on the pattern equal 1". For a smaller indoor sign, let each square equal ½". Transfer the pattern to the sign stock, and cut it out with a band saw or saber saw. Round over the edges slightly and sand them to remove the saw marks.

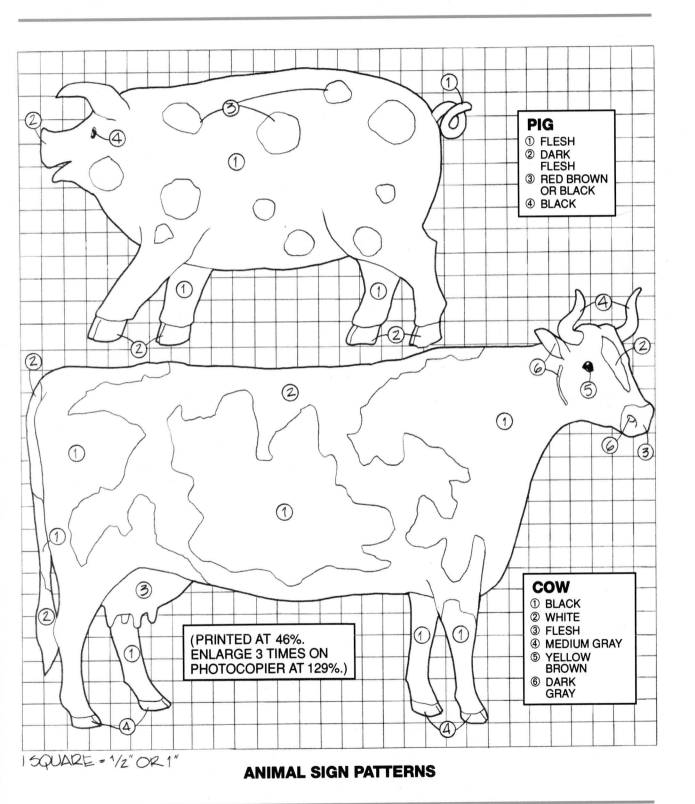

PIG
① FLESH
② DARK FLESH
③ RED BROWN OR BLACK
④ BLACK

COW
① BLACK
② WHITE
③ FLESH
④ MEDIUM GRAY
⑤ YELLOW BROWN
⑥ DARK GRAY

(PRINTED AT 46%. ENLARGE 3 TIMES ON PHOTOCOPIER AT 129%.)

1 SQUARE = ½" OR 1"

ANIMAL SIGN PATTERNS

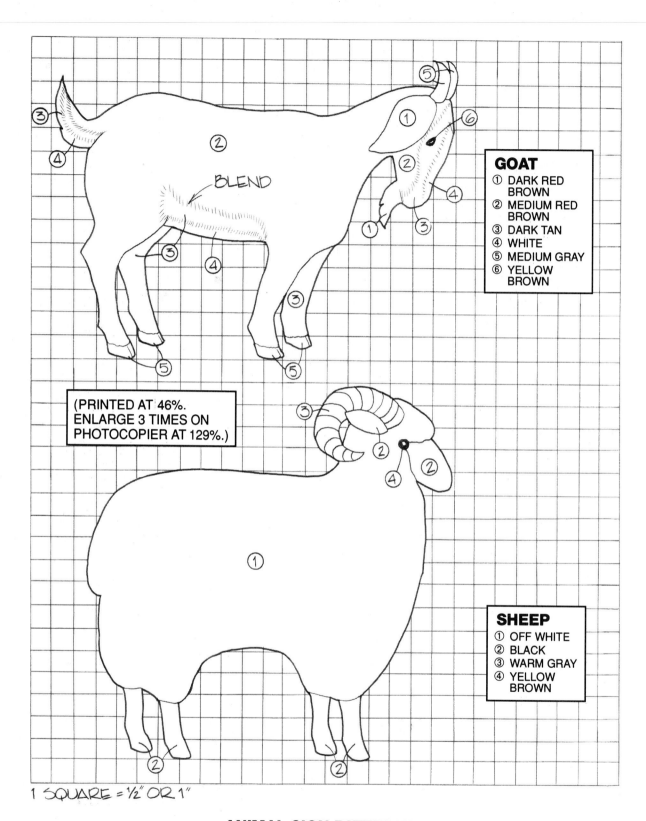

GOAT
① DARK RED BROWN
② MEDIUM RED BROWN
③ DARK TAN
④ WHITE
⑤ MEDIUM GRAY
⑥ YELLOW BROWN

BLEND

(PRINTED AT 46%. ENLARGE 3 TIMES ON PHOTOCOPIER AT 129%.)

SHEEP
① OFF WHITE
② BLACK
③ WARM GRAY
④ YELLOW BROWN

1 SQUARE = ½" OR 1"

ANIMAL SIGN PATTERNS

If you're making a hex sign, cut a large circle. The circle can be any diameter — some old barn signs were 4' across. The size will depend on where you want to display the sign. Choose one of the illustrated hex patterns. Here are some possible interpretations of the symbols:

■ The *rosette* will keep bad luck away from you. The ocean ring promotes smooth sailing throughout your life.

■ The *five-pointed star* brings you good luck. The raindrops and the sun ring provide the good weather needed to make your endeavors blossom and bear fruit.

■ The *six-pointed star* will protect your house, barn, or shop (and the occupants) from lightning and other disasters. The sun ring brings you many bright days.

■ The *eight-pointed star* brings you an abundance of good things in your life. The tulips will keep your faith strong, and the hearts help you love your fellowman and show him goodwill.

If none of these fit your particular needs, or you want to design your own hex sign, consult The Picture Language of Hex Signs at the end of this chapter. When you have chosen or made up a design, transfer it to the stock.

3 *Paint the sign.* If you intend to display the sign outdoors (and want it to remain new-looking), coat it with a clear, petroleum-based water seal. Otherwise, don't prime the stock or prepare it in any other way. The paint covers more easily and adheres better when applied to raw wood.

Color the signs with latex or acrylic paint. Follow the color codes on the drawings, or choose your own colors. If you're painting an animal sign, you may want to get a picture book of farm animals from the library. Use this as a guide while you work. If you're painting a hex sign, use vivid, bright colors. Avoid pastels and earth tones.

For a new-looking sign, apply the paint conventionally. To imitate a weathered look, apply the paint with what artists call a "dry brush." When you dip the brush in a color, load just a little paint on the tip. Wipe off most of the paint on paper or scrap wood until the

brush is relatively dry, then apply what little remains to the sign. This technique lets you apply a very thin coat of color. Done properly, the finished piece looks as if most of the paint has weathered away. If you get the paint too thick in any one spot, wipe it off with a damp cloth.

After the paint dries, coat it with a clear protective finish. If you want to display the sign outdoors, use a UV-resistant polyurethane or spar varnish. If it's an indoor sign, apply shellac or lacquer. To make a painted sign look old, mix a little burnt umber artist's oil color with the finish before you apply it. This will tone down the colors, making them appear timeworn. To determine the amount of burnt umber needed for a specific amount of finish, experiment with a piece of scrap wood. You probably won't have to use more than a few drops per pint.

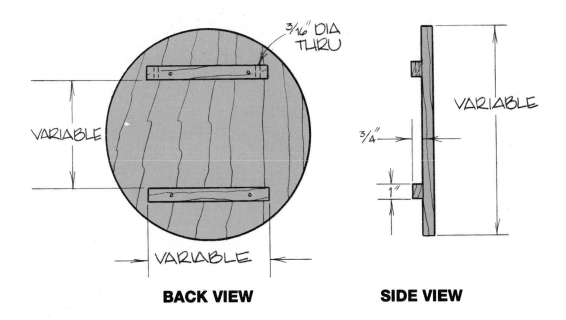

BACK VIEW   **SIDE VIEW**

① PALE YELLOW
② ORANGE
③ BRIGHT YELLOW
④ BRIGHT GREEN
⑤ MEDIUM GREEN
⑥ LIGHT BLUE
⑦ WHITE
⑧ DARK GREEN

① RUST RED
② LIGHT TURQUOISE
③ YELLOW
④ GOLD
⑤ ORANGE
⑥ BLACK
⑦ CREAM WHITE
⑧ RUST BROWN

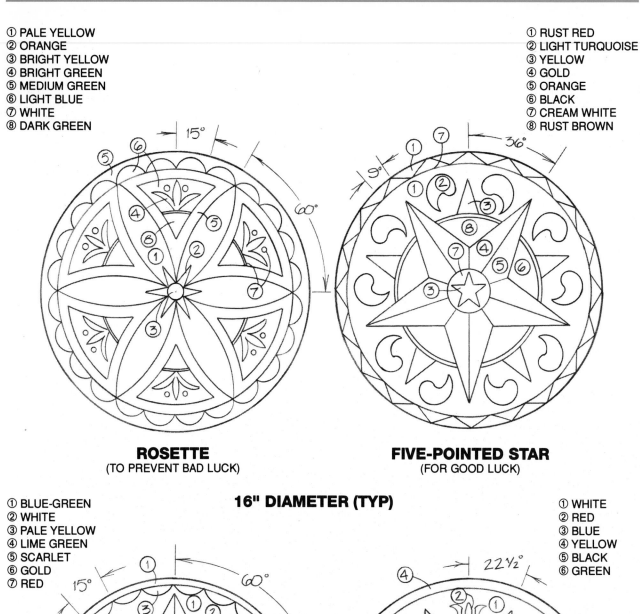

ROSETTE
(TO PREVENT BAD LUCK)

FIVE-POINTED STAR
(FOR GOOD LUCK)

16" DIAMETER (TYP)

① BLUE-GREEN
② WHITE
③ PALE YELLOW
④ LIME GREEN
⑤ SCARLET
⑥ GOLD
⑦ RED

① WHITE
② RED
③ BLUE
④ YELLOW
⑤ BLACK
⑥ GREEN

SIX-POINTED STAR
(TO PROTECT AGAINST DISASTER)

EIGHT-POINTED STAR
(FOR ABUNDANCE AND GOODWILL)

4 **Hang the sign.** If you hang the sign indoors, install two eye screws in the back, near the top, on opposite sides. Stretch picture hanging wire between them. Use a sufficiently thick gauge of wire to support the weight of the sign. Hang the sign from a nail or a picture hook.

To hang the sign on the outside of a house or out-building, make two long, narrow brackets. Drill two ³⁄₁₆"-diameter holes in one of the brackets, one hole near each end. (If the sign is very large, drill a third hole near the middle.) Screw the brackets to the back of the sign, placing one bracket (the one with holes) near the top and the other near the bottom.

Drive L-hooks into the side of the building, at the precise spacing of the holes in the upper bracket. Hang the sign temporarily, slipping the upper bracket over the L-hooks. Mark where the *top* edge of the lower bracket rests against the building. Remove the sign, and screw the stop blocks to the building, placing the *bottom* edges of the blocks even with the marks you made.

Hang the sign again, holding the bottom edge out from the building while you slip the upper bracket over the hooks. Then push the bottom edge against the building, slipping the lower bracket beneath the stop blocks. (See Figure 1.) This arrangement keeps the sign in place, even during a strong wind. It also lets you remove the sign easily, should you need to paint or repair the building.

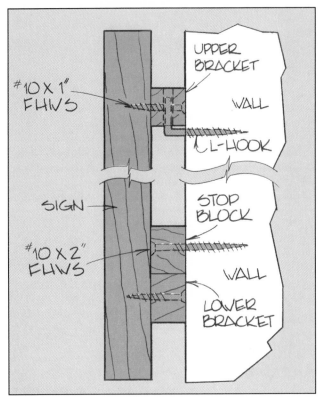

1/When hanging a sign on a home or an outbuilding, suspend it from L-hooks driven into the wall. Use stop blocks to keep the sign from coming off the hooks during bad weather.

The Picture Language of Hex Signs

Much controversy surrounds hex signs. Some folklorists argue that the signs are composed of ancient symbols, each with a special meaning for the Germanic peoples who devised them. When combined within a circle, the symbols have the power to bring good luck and ward off evil. Other scholars contend that the signs are only decorative; if the symbols had any meaning, they have long ago been lost.

The historical evidence supports both views. In the Dark Ages, the inhabitants of the Rhine Valley developed a system of religious and superstitious symbols. Some were the signs of the new Christian believers. (Charlemagne's armies had recently conquered and forcefully converted the Germans.) Others were derived from their traditional pagan worship of Wotan (or Oden). They painted these symbols on furniture, doors, fireplaces, and other parts of their homes. These early hex signs were small and usually displayed indoors.

Over the centuries, the symbols lost their significance and became more traditional than meaningful. When immigrants from the Rhine valley began to settle in southeastern Pennsylvania, they still decorated their furniture with hearts and tulips and distelfinks, but few believed in the power of the old signs. In the late nineteenth century, when it became fashionable to embellish buildings with bright colors and intricate designs, some Pennsylvania Dutch began to paint the signs on their barns. For the first time, the symbols were prominently displayed outside. When a passerby would stop and ask about the strange, geometric designs on a barn, the owner would respond that his ancestors once considered them to be powerful charms. This began the legend (and the controversy) of hex signs.

It's difficult to establish the original meanings of all the symbols, since sources often conflict. However, there is general agreement on several points.

Continued

The Picture Language of Hex Signs — Continued

For one, every hex sign starts with a circle — the circle of life or "witch's circle." The symbols have no power unless placed inside the circumference. The signs are often used in multiples and arranged in a symmetrical or geometrical pattern. This reflects the divine order of creation. Most symbols have multiple meanings, and these may change when used in combination with other symbols. For example, a blue ocean border is a charm for smooth passage through the ups and downs of life. You might put hearts within that border to smooth out the ups and downs of marriage.

There are no rules that determine the specific meaning of a combination of symbols. This is left up to the person who paints and uses the hex sign. Should you wish to design your own hex sign, here is a list of common symbols and their possible meanings.

Rosette — Prevents bad fortune, and keeps the devil and his servants from entering a building. This is perhaps the most ancient of all hex symbols. Many early Christian churches had round windows with painted or carved rosettes.

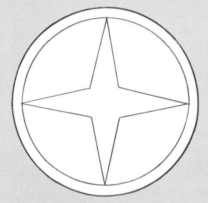

Four-pointed star — Sometimes called the "morning star," it brings enlightenment or bright, new beginnings. It may also allude to the four seasons (summer, fall, winter, and spring) or the four cardinal points of the compass (north, south, east, and west).

Five-pointed star — Also called the "lucky star," it brings good fortune. When used in threes, it fosters good luck, success, and happiness.

Six-pointed star — Similar to the rosette. It prevents damage from lightning strikes, floods, tornadoes, and other natural disasters. It can also prevent disease.

Eight-pointed star — Promotes abundance or prosperity. The eight points refer to the four seasons and the four elements (earth, air, fire, and water).

Raindrops — Bring rain; also encourage fertility. These are often used within the sun border to bring good growing conditions and a plentiful harvest.

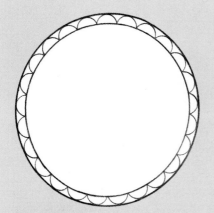

Ocean border — Provides a safe, smooth passage through the ups and downs of life.

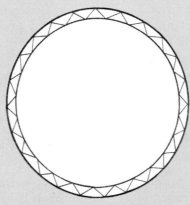

Sun border — Brings sunny days, good weather, or happiness.

Distelfink — Means "thistle finch" in German. This bird is a harbinger of good fortune.

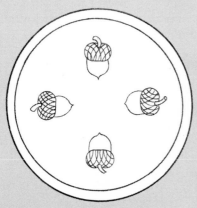

Acorns — Represent children, family, or eternal life.

Hearts — Promote love, romance, marriage, charity, or goodwill.

Serpent — Protects against temptation.

Oak leaves — Promote good health and strength of character. If the leaves are painted in autumn colors, they may also sustain health and happiness in old age.

Tulips — Represent faith. These are actually stylized holy lilies. The three points on each flower allude to the triumvirate nature of God (Father, Son, and Holy Ghost).

Crescent moons — Promote growth, progress, or a change for the better. Four moons may refer to the four seasons.

Pull Toys

There have been toys with wheels since ancient times. But for much of recorded history these were rare; most playthings were simple miniatures without means of movement. Only since the early nineteenth century have pull toys become commonplace. The Industrial Revolution created an interest in locomotion, and children became increasingly fascinated with playthings that moved or rolled.

The animal pull toys shown are typical of the late 1800s. Parents made or bought moving animals of all sorts for their children — farm animals, circus animals, and household pets. Rams and goats were especially popular. During the Victorian era, folks trained goats to pull small carriages or carry children on their backs. A child of the late nineteenth century might have wished for a ram at Christmas for the same reason a present-day youngster longs for a pony.

Some pull toys did more than just roll. The maker harnessed the motion of the wheels to create some other sound or movement. On "rolling ball" toys, four large wheels turned a ball that rested between them. The balls were painted with happy and sad faces, pinwheels, or multicolored designs. The ball shown is carved and painted to look like a dog. As the toy is pulled forward, the dog appears to somersault backward.

**RAM PULL TOY
EXPLODED VIEW**

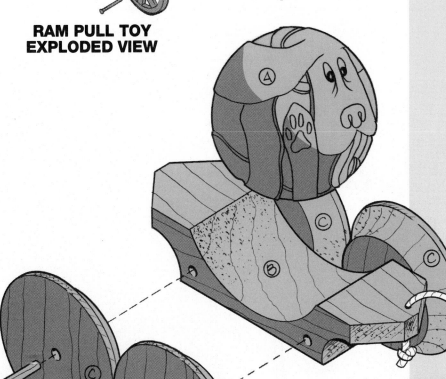

**ROLLING ROVER
EXPLODED VIEW**

Materials List

FINISHED DIMENSIONS

PARTS

Ram Pull Toy

A.	Body	1½" x 5¼" x 6¾"
B.	Legs (4)	⅜" dia. x 1¾"
C.	Base	½" x 3½" x 9"
D.	Bead	1" dia.
E.	Plug	½" dia. x ¼"

Rolling Rover

A.	Ball	5" dia.
B.	Cart	1⅝" x 2¾" x 9"
C.	Wheels (4)	4" dia. x ¾"
D.	Axle pegs (4)	½" dia. x 1¾"
E.	Bead	1" dia.
F.	Plug	½" dia. x ¼"

HARDWARE

Ram Pull Toy
2" Metal wheels and axle-nails with flat
   washers (4)
³/₁₆" Nylon rope (36")

Rolling Rover
³/₁₆" Nylon rope (36")

Making the Ram Pull Toy

1 ***Select the stock and cut it to size.***
Since this toy will be painted, choose light-colored woods. Make the body of the ram from something that's easy to carve, such as basswood or butternut. Make the other parts from harder woods, such as maple or birch. All of these woods are fairly durable, and they provide a good painting surface. The natural wood tones are almost white, so the colors that are painted over them remain vivid.

After selecting the stock, plane it to the thicknesses needed — 1½" for the body and ½" for the base. Cut the parts to size.

2 ***Transfer the patterns to the stock.***
Enlarge the *Ram Patterns,* and transfer them to the body stock. Trace the side pattern on a face of the stock and the front pattern on an end. Check that the patterns are aligned properly. The base or lowest part of each pattern should be even with the bottom edge of the stock.

FRONT VIEW   **SIDE VIEW**

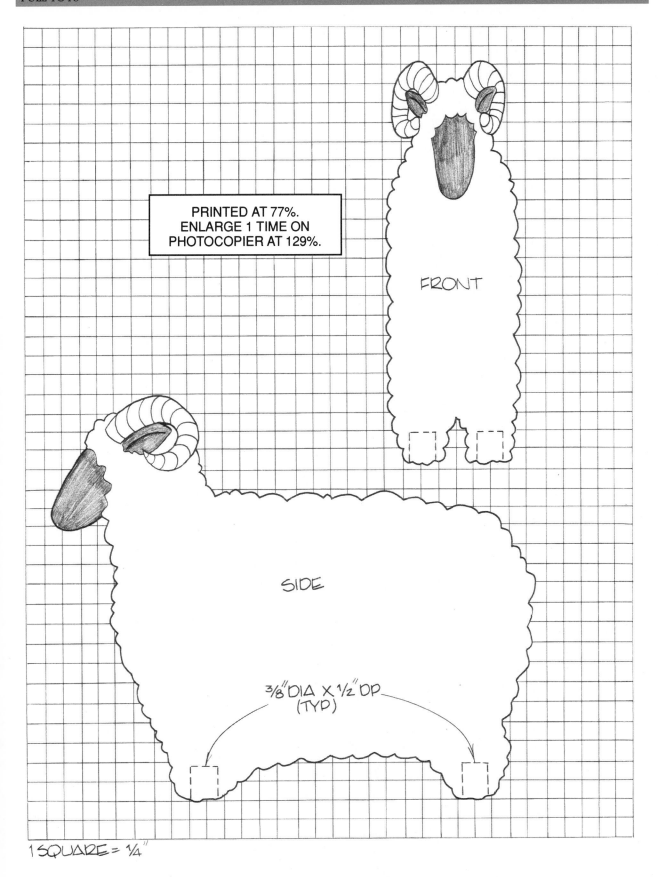

PRINTED AT 77%.
ENLARGE 1 TIME ON
PHOTOCOPIER AT 129%.

FRONT

SIDE

³⁄₈" DIA X ½" DP
(TYP)

1 SQUARE = ¼"

RAM PATTERNS

3 *Drill the holes in the body, base, and bead.*

Mark the locations of the stopped holes for the legs. Make certain that these marks line up with the ram's legs in the patterns, then drill four ⅜"-diameter, ½"-deep holes in the bottom of the body stock.

While you're working at the drill press, make the holes needed to attach the rope to the base and the bead. First, drill ½"-diameter counterbores, as shown in the *Base Detail* and *Bead Detail*. These counterbores will hold the knots on the ends of the rope. Drill ³⁄₁₆"-diameter holes through the centers of the counterbores to insert the rope.

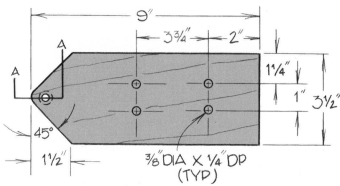
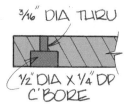

BASE DETAIL

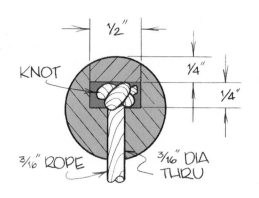

BEAD DETAIL

SECTION A

4 *Cut the shape of the ram and the base.*

Rough out the shape of the ram with a band saw. Cut the front (end) pattern first, saving the waste. (See Figure 1.) Tape the waste back to the workpiece and cut the side (face) pattern. (See Figure 2.) When you remove the tape and the waste, you'll have a rough — but unmistakable — ram shape.

Note: The capacity of some home workshop band saws is too small to saw the body stock lengthwise, making it impossible to cut the front pattern. If this is the case, don't worry. Cut the side pattern only. The front pattern isn't essential; it just saves you time when you carve the ram.

After cutting the ram shape, mark the shape of the base. Cut it on the band saw, then sand the sawed edges.

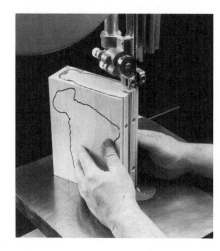

1/Rough shape the body of the ram by making a compound cut on your band saw. First, cut the front pattern, with the block resting on its end. Save the waste.

2/Tape the waste back to the workpiece. Cut the side pattern with the block resting on its face. After you remove the tape and the waste, you'll have the rough shape of a ram.

5 *Drill the leg holes in the base.* Place

dowel centers in the holes you drilled in the body. Center the body on the base side to side, and place the rear legs 2" from the back edge. Press down hard on the body, or tap it with a mallet, so the dowel centers leave small indentations in the base. (See Figure 3.) Drill a ⅜"-diameter, ¼"-deep hole at each indentation.

3/Place the dowel centers in the body and press the body down on the base. The dowel centers will leave small indentations. To make these more visible, rub the dowel centers with a soft pencil before you press the body against the base.

6 *Carve the shape of the ram.* Using a

carving knife, round over the edges of the body. This will give it a more natural shape. Carve the features of the head — nose, horns, and ears. Don't worry if you are an inexperienced carver; the shapes don't have to be realistic. In fact, they should be fairly rough. A country craftsman wouldn't have spent the time to make a realistic sculpture for children. He would have roughed out the shape and expected them to fill in the details with their imaginations.

To create the impression of wool, cut V-shaped grooves, ¼"–½" long, over most of the body with a parting tool (sometimes called a corner chisel). Make these grooves in pairs, curving each groove slightly, so one nestles inside the other. (See Figures 4 and 5.) Continue until you have covered the entire body with these grooves *except* the nose, ears, and horns.

4/Using a parting tool, cut small grooves over most of the body of the ram to imitate the texture of wool. Don't cut grooves where there is no wool, or where the wool is very short — the nose, ears, and horns.

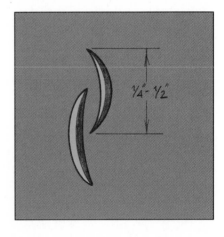

¼"– ½"

5/Make the grooves in pairs, as shown, curving them in opposite directions.

7 *Assemble the body, legs, and base.*

Finish sand the base and legs. Glue the legs in the body, then in the base. Use a generous amount of glue, and wipe away any excess that squeezes out with a wet rag.

8 *Paint the ram.* Do any necessary touch-up

sanding, then paint the ram assembly with latex or acrylic paint. Color the base green, the horns tan, and the legs, ears, and nose black. If you want, paint the woolly parts of the body a cream white. Or you can leave them unpainted, since the wood is cream-colored already. After the paint dries, apply a coat of tung oil. This will harden the paint and protect unpainted areas.

9

Attach the wheels, rope, and bead.
Drill ¹⁄₁₆"-diameter pilot holes for the axle-nails that will hold the wheels to the base. Insert the nails through the wheel hubs and put a small flat washer over the shaft of each nail. (These washers will keep the metal wheels from rubbing on the wooden base.) Attach the wheels to the base, carefully tapping the nails into the wood. Tap the nails until the wheels no longer wobble but still turn freely.

Insert the end of the rope through the ³⁄₁₆"-diameter hole in the bead. Tie a knot in the end of the rope and pull it back through the hole, so the knot nests in the ½"-diameter counterbore. Glue a plug in the counterbore, covering the knot. When the glue dries, sand and file the end of the plug flush with the surface of the bead. Paint or apply a finish to the bead.

Insert the other end of the rope down through the ³⁄₁₆"-diameter hole in the pointed end of the base. Tie a knot in the end and nest it in the counterbore, as you did with the bead. If you wish, put a few drops of glue on the knot to keep it in the counterbore.

Making Rolling Rover

1

Select the stock and cut it to size.
When choosing stock for the rolling ball pull toy, use the same criteria as for the ram. Select light-colored, durable hardwoods. Use basswood or butternut for the ball — these are easy to carve. Make the cart, wheels, and other parts from harder woods, such as maple or birch. You can purchase the axle pegs ready-made from most woodworking suppliers. If you wish to make them yourself, buy ½"-diameter hardwood dowel stock.

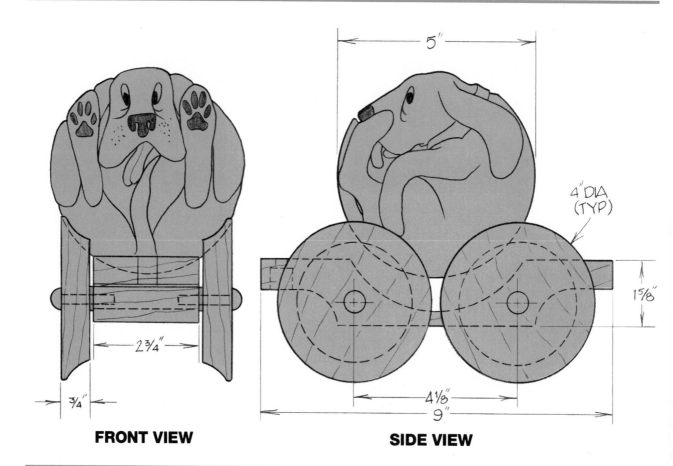

FRONT VIEW　　　　**SIDE VIEW**

Plane the stock to the thicknesses needed for the cart assembly — 1½" for the cart, and ¾" for the wheels. Cut the parts to the sizes needed. Glue up a turning block, 5¼" x 5¼" x 8", to make the ball.

Warning: When gluing up lathe stock, let the glue cure for *at least* 24 hours before turning the wood. If you don't allow the glue to dry completely, the stock may come apart on the lathe.

2 **Make the cart.** Lay out the side profile on the edge of the cart stock. Measure and mark the positions of the axle holes on both edges. At each mark, drill a ⁵⁄₁₆"-diameter hole, ¾" deep.

Cut the profile of the cart on a band saw. Then turn the cart upside down and mark the ends and the rope hole, as shown in the *Cart/Top View.* Cut the shape of the ends. To make the rope hole, first drill a ½"-diameter counterbore, ⅜" deep. Then drill a ³⁄₁₆"-diameter hole through the center of the counterbore. Sand the sawed edges of the cart.

3 **Make the wheels.** Cut each wheel slightly oversize and drill a ⅜"-diameter axle hole through the center. Then mount the wheel on the lathe. To do this, you first have to make a set of ¾" x 1½" x 1½" blocks, as shown in the *Pressure Turning Blocks* drawing. Drill a ⅜"-diameter, ⅜"-deep hole in the center of each block, then drill a ⅛"-diameter hole the rest of the way through the center. Cut a ⅜"-diameter dowel, 1¼" long, to fit in the ⅜"-diameter hole.

Place the wheel between the blocks, with the dowel through the axle hole. Mount this assembly between the centers of the lathe, with the points of the centers in the ⅛"-diameter holes. (See Figure 1.) The pressure between the centers will keep the assembly together on the lathe.

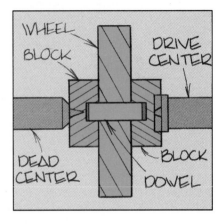

1/Mount the wheel on the lathe, pressed between two wooden blocks. (Stock turned in that manner is sometimes called a pressure turning.) A dowel through the axle hole centers the wheels.

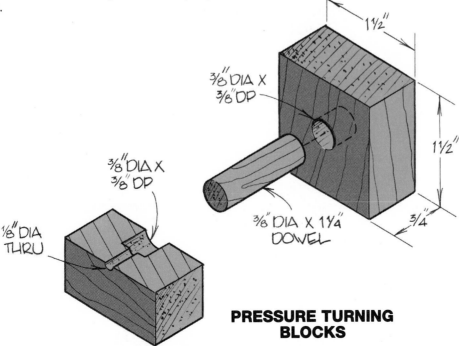

PRESSURE TURNING BLOCKS

Turn the wheel, cutting a cove in one edge, as shown in the *Wheel Profile*. (See Figure 2.) On the assembled project, this cove becomes a cradle for the ball. Turn the circumference of the wheel to precisely 4", then round over any sharp edges. Finally, sand the wheel on the lathe. Repeat this procedure for the other wheels.

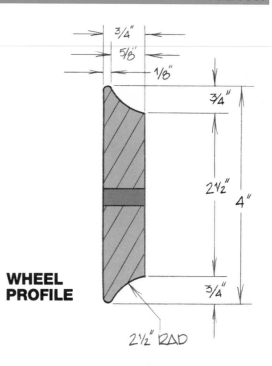

WHEEL PROFILE

2/Cut a cove in the edge of the wheel. Feed the gouge very slowly. Because the grain of the wheel is perpendicular to rotation, the tool will catch if you feed it too quickly.

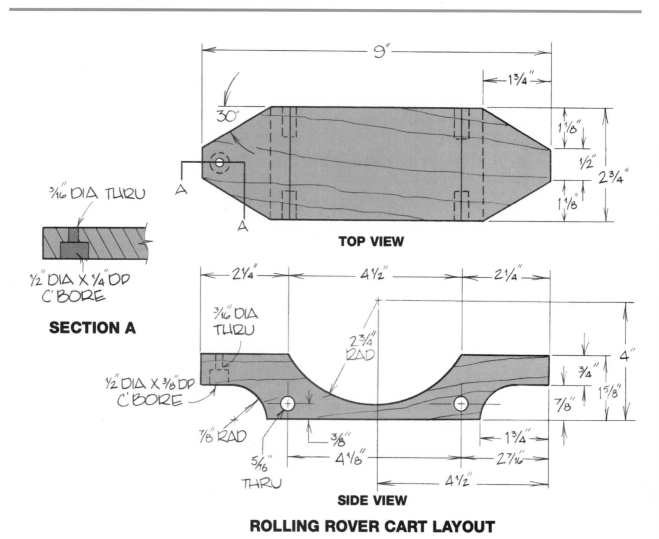

TOP VIEW

³⁄₁₆" DIA THRU

½" DIA X ¼" DP
C'BORE

SECTION A

SIDE VIEW

ROLLING ROVER CART LAYOUT

4 **Turn the ball.** Mount the ball stock between the lathe centers and turn a sphere. To help turn a perfectly round sphere exactly 5" in diameter, make a template from ¼" plywood, as shown in the *Ball Template Layout*. Carefully turn the waste at either end of the ball to 1" in diameter. *Don't turn it any smaller!* Then begin to turn the ball. As the ball approaches a spherical shape, stop the turning occasionally and compare it to the template. (See Figure 3.) Pare away the high spots until the template fits over the ball.

Sand the ball on the lathe. Remove it, cut off the waste, and sand the ends. Be careful not to flatten the ends as you smooth them. However, don't be concerned if the turning is not perfectly spherical when you're finished. The toy will work just fine even if there are a few high and low spots on the ball.

3/Use a plywood template to gauge the shape and diameter of the ball as you turn it. Be careful not to turn the waste at either end of the ball smaller than 1" in diameter. If you do, the ball will be egg-shaped.

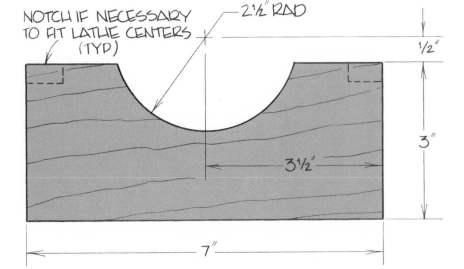

NOTCH IF NECESSARY TO FIT LATHE CENTERS (TYP)

2½" RAD

½"

3"

3½"

7"

BALL TEMPLATE LAYOUT

5 **Transfer the pattern to the ball.** Enlarge the *Ball Pattern*. Make several full-size copies; you may need them. Scribble on the back of the full-size pattern with a soft pencil, completely covering it with lead. Cut out the pattern and tape *one* of the oval-shaped sections to the ball. Then tape the points of all the sections together, bending the pattern around the ball. The pattern will completely cover the ball, like the peel of an orange. (See Figure 4.) With a ballpoint pen, trace the lines of the dog. Press hard, so the lead on the back of the pattern transfers to the wooden surface.

Remove the tape and unwrap the pattern. Clean up the lines on the ball, making them heavier and smoothing out any zigs or zags that don't look right. Don't worry if your Rover doesn't appear exactly like the one shown. This will just serve to make it distinctive.

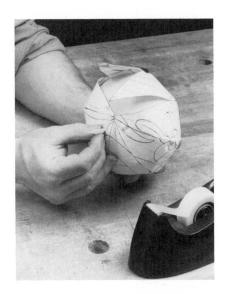

4/Wrap the pattern around the ball, like an orange peel. If the pattern does not fit, measure the diameter of the ball. It may be too big or too small. If this is the case, you will have to adjust the percentage of enlargement to fit the ball. Enlarge the pattern again, using the traditional squares method.

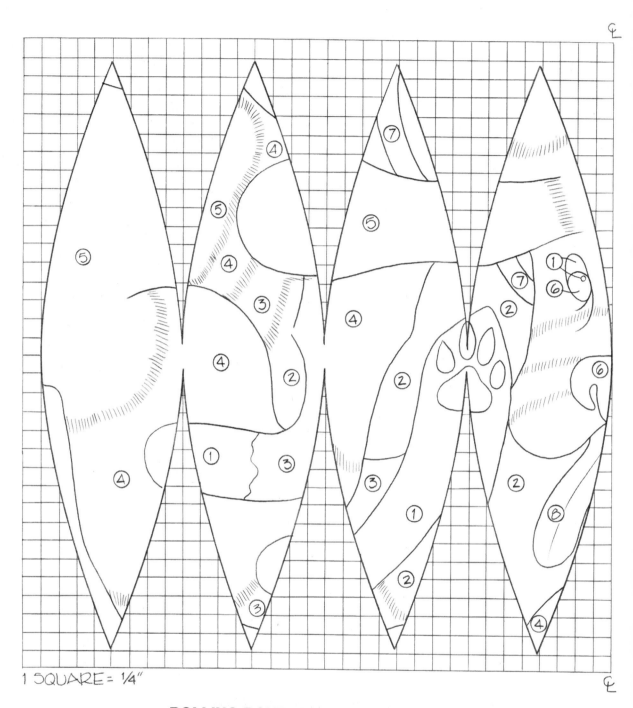

1 SQUARE = ¼"

ROLLING ROVER/BALL PATTERN

(PRINTED AT 77%.
ENLARGE 1 TIME ON
PHOTOCOPIER AT 129%.)

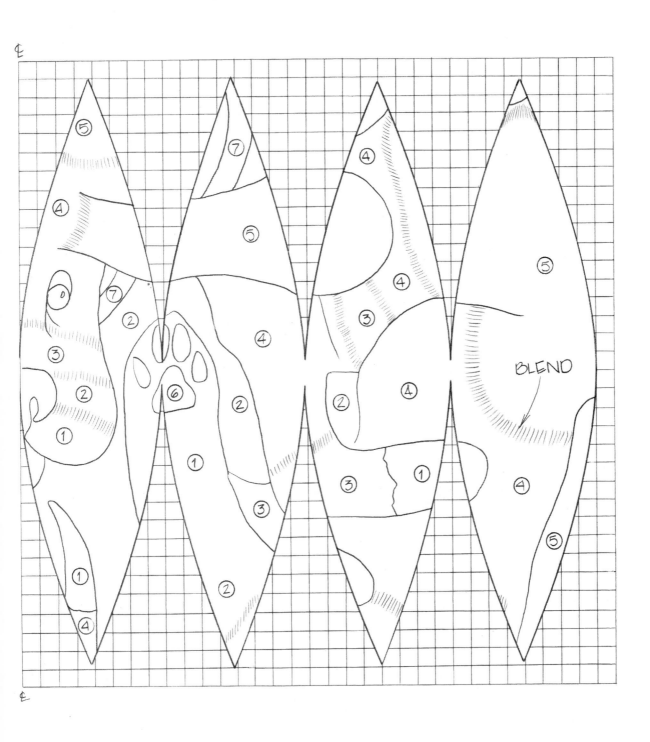

① WHITE
② LIGHT TAN
③ LIGHT RED BROWN
④ MEDIUM RED BROWN
⑤ DARK RED BROWN
⑥ BLACK
⑦ DARK TURQUOISE
⑧ RED

DARK RED BROWN
LIGHTENED SUCCESSIVELY
INTO FOUR SHADES

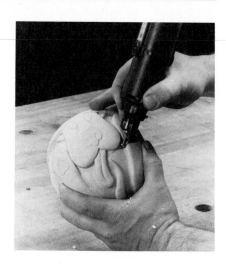

6 **Carve the ball.** *Lightly* carve the shape of the dog. Don't cut too deep — no more than ½" in any one area. If you remove too much stock, the ball won't roll properly on the wheels. Remember that the dog shape is really just a bas-relief carving wrapped around a spherical surface. Proceed as you would for ordinary bas-relief work: Outline the shapes with a chisel, then remove just enough stock to give the dog some dimension. (See Figure 5.)

Sand the carving to remove any chisel or machine marks. If you have accidentally removed too much stock at any one point, fill the area with an epoxy-based wood putty. After the putty hardens, file or sand it to the desired depth and contour.

5/If you have a flexible shaft tool or a miniature router, you can use it to help rough out the carving. These tools remove stock much more quickly than knives and chisels. However, because of this, you'll have to be that much more careful not to remove too much stock.

7 **Assemble the cart.** If you haven't bought ready-made axle pegs, turn them from ½" dowel stock as shown in the *Axle Peg Detail*. Do any touch-up sanding needed on the parts of the cart, then insert an axle peg through the hole in each wheel. Spread glue on the end of each peg and in each axle hole. Tap the pegs into the holes with a mallet. Remember that the wheels must turn freely. Drive the pegs until they are just tight enough to hold the wheels close to the cart without binding.

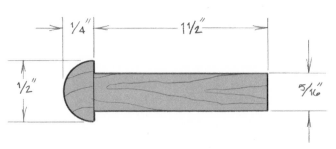

AXLE PEG DETAIL

8 **Paint the cart and the dog.** Paint all the wood surfaces with latex or acrylic paint. Follow the color codes on the drawings, or choose your own colors. You may wish to get a picture book on dogs from the library and use it as a guide when you paint the ball. Turn to the pictures of beagles — Rolling Rover is a caricature of a beagle.

9 **Attach the rope and bead.** Attach the rope and bead as described for the ram pull toy. Insert the ends of the rope through the ³⁄₁₆"-diameter holes in the bead and cart. Knot the ends, then nest the knots in the counterbores. Plug the bead counterbore, covering the knot. Sand the bead, then paint it or apply a finish.

Burled Bowls and Cups

Country folk once prized bowls, cups, and other containers made of burled wood, because burls are dense and hard enough to endure heavy use. The wood grain is tightly packed and does not absorb moisture easily, so a bowl can be washed or filled with liquids. There is no real grain direction — the grain goes in every direction — so the wood doesn't expand and contract unevenly. This reduces the chance that a bowl will warp or crack.

You can find burled wood in every tree. On some trees, particularly older ones, you'll find it in large, wartlike formations on the sides of trunks and limbs. On most trees, however, it's not quite so evident. The burls are below the ground in the tap root — the large root that points almost straight down, in the opposite direction of the trunk. Country turners often dug up the stumps of giant walnut and maple trees to get these roots.

The bowl, cup, and covered jar shown were turned by Robert S. Pinter, a professional woodworker from Tipp City, Ohio. The bowl and the jar are of his own design, while the cup is a copy of an old Shaker dipper cup. Much of the information in this chapter comes from Rude Osolnik, a master woodturner from Berea, Kentucky. Rude (pronounced Rudy) is a retired professor of wood arts at Berea College. He now teaches seminars in woodturning all across the country.

Note: There are no Materials Lists for these projects. Because they are turned from a single piece of wood, there are no parts in the usual sense. Nor are there any specific measurements or patterns. The size and shape of each turning depends on the size and shape of the burl it's made from. ●

1 Harvest and prepare a burl.

Harvest and prepare a burl. You can't buy burled wood at a lumberyard, but you can obtain it from many different sources, if you look around. For instance, you (or a friend of yours) may have a tree with a large burl on the side of its trunk. If you're careful, you can cut this out with a chainsaw and not hurt the tree. Don't cut too deeply, and paint the wound with pruning tar to prevent the tree from becoming infested or diseased. In time, the wound will heal over. It may even develop another burl that your grandchildren can harvest.

If you can't locate a burl on a trunk or limb, look underground. You may find a stump that you can dig up. Farmers often harvest the mature trees in their woodlots. After the loggers take the farmer's trees down, you can usually get a stump or two for little or nothing. Most farmers are glad to have you haul them away.

Once you have procured a burl, prepare it for turning. There are two common methods. The first is to soak it in a vat of polyethylene glycol (PEG) for several months. PEG slowly replaces the water in the wood fibers, chemically drying the wood. Unlike water, PEG doesn't evaporate and the wood won't shrink, distort, or split.

But PEG has limitations. For one thing, it's not cheap. And you need a vat that's big enough to soak the burl, and a place to store the vat. Finally, you have to use specially prepared finishes, since the oily PEG never dries. As you might guess, these finishes are all fairly expensive.

Rude Osolnik uses an inexpensive alternative — plastic bags. Wood splits because it dries unevenly; the surface loses moisture before the interior. Once Rude starts to turn a burl, he stores it in a plastic bag. This slows the evaporation of moisture from the newly exposed surface.

2 Round the burl on the lathe.

Round the burl on the lathe. Cut away any unwanted stock from the burl with a band saw. Estimate the turning axis and mount the burl between the lathe centers, as if it were a spindle turning. Set the lathe to run at its lowest speed, and turn it on. If there's too much vibration, turn the lathe off *immediately*. Adjust the position of the centers, and try again.

When the burl will turn without vibrating overmuch, begin rounding the outside. As you work, check that you're not removing more stock from one side of the turning than the other. If you are, you haven't found the true axis yet. Dismount the turning and move one of the lathe centers ¼"–½" *away* from the side that isn't being shaved by the chisel. (See Figure 1.) If necessary, experiment with several different center positions until you find one that suits you. When you're satisfied, round the outside of the burl to create a rough bowl shape.

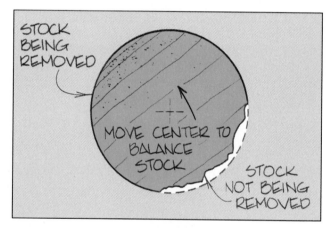

1/If the lathe centers are positioned improperly, you will remove more stock from one side of the burl than the other. This wastes good stock. Relocate one center a short distance away from the side that's **not** being shaved by the chisel.

3 Turn a tenon at the base of the bowl.

Turn a tenon at the base of the bowl. Mount the burl on a faceplate to complete the outside shape of the bowl and turn the inside shape. To keep the same turning axis that you worked so hard to find, you must attach the burl to the faceplate in the same position (relative to the lathe) that it occupied between the centers. Preserve this axis by first turning a round tenon at the base of the bowl shape. Then insert the tenon in the mounting hole of the faceplate, and screw the faceplate to the burl. (See Figures 2, 3, and 4.)

Mount the faceplate on the lathe, and advance the tailstock to see where the live center meets the burl. If the axis has been preserved, the center will contact the burl in the same place as before. Don't worry if the contact point has moved slightly; this is normal.

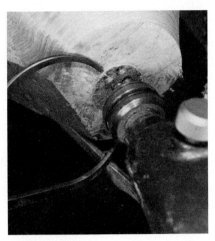

2/To transfer a rough-shaped bowl to a faceplate, first measure the diameter of the faceplate mounting hole with calipers.

3/Turn a short, round tenon at the base of the bowl. This tenon must be exactly the same diameter as the faceplate mounting hole.

4/Mount the turning to the faceplate, inserting the round tenon in the mounting hole. This will help you keep the same turning axis that you worked

with when the stock was mounted as a spindle turning.

4
Finish turning the outside shape of the bowl. If you are turning a large burl, leave the tailstock and live center in place, pressed hard against the stock. This will provide extra support while you turn.

As you finish turning the outside shape, inspect the surface for checks and cracks. You'll often find small imperfections in the wood that weren't visible when you began. You must fill these; if you let them go, they may eventually ruin the bowl. One of the strongest filling materials (and one of the easiest to apply) is cyanoacrylate glue. This glue comes in two parts — resin and activator. Apply the resin first, then the activator. Immediately, the glue expands to seal the cavity and begins to harden. It's hard enough to begin turning again in a few minutes. (See Figure 5.) Cyanoacrylate glue is available from several mail-order woodworking suppliers, or you can buy it from:

Hot Stuff Glue
Satellite City
P.O. Box 836
Simi, CA 93062

After you finish shaping the outside of the bowl, rough sand the turning. Make sure you sand any glue flush to the surface of the wood.

TRY THIS! Cyanoacrylate glue is also useful for hardening the rotted parts of spalted woods. These woods are laced with black lines that form intriguing patterns when a piece is turned. Unfortunately, the lines are created by the same bacteria that cause the wood to rot.

5/Fill small checks or cracks with cyanoacrylate glue to keep them from getting bigger. If the checks are too big, and they continue to pull apart as you turn the bowl, you may have to discard the burl.

5

Turn the inside of the bowl. The hardest part of turning the inside of a bowl is knowing when to stop. The second hardest part is turning the very center, because the stock wants to catch the chisel and whip it around. To solve both of these problems, mount a drill chuck on the tailstock. Secure a 1"-diameter Forstner bit or multispur bit in the chuck, then drill a hole down the center of the burl. (See Figure 6.) Monitor the depth of the hole as you drill it, and stop when the bit reaches the bottom of the bowl.

Pare away the inside of the bowl, working from the outside edge toward the center hole. Stop when you get to the bottom of the center hole. Try to cut the sides as thin as possible, using less and less pressure on the chisel as you remove more stock from the sides. But don't cut the sides so thin that they become fragile. A good burled bowl is light *and* durable.

*6/To establish the depth of a bowl turning, drill a 1"-diameter hole down the center. Consider the length of the screws that attach the burl to the faceplate. If the screws penetrate 1" into the stock, stop the hole 1½" to 1¾" short of the faceplate. You want to leave enough waste at the base of the turning so you can cut it free **without** cutting through a screw.*

TRY THIS! When turning very large bowls, consider turning the lip *inside*, making what some turners call a "reverse curve." This shape strengthens the sides of the bowl and helps prevent distortion.

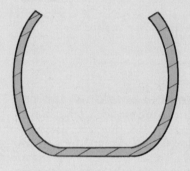

TYPICAL REVERSE CURVE

6

Finish sand the bowl. Finish sand the completed bowl, inside and out, on the lathe. Let the friction of the sandpaper warm the sides of the bowl as you sand. This will evaporate the remaining water in the wood, drying the bowl to a moisture content of 10–15 percent — the same range as most air-dried lumber.

However, *don't let the surface of the wood get too hot!* If the water evaporates too quickly, the sides may check or split. To help prevent this, work with sharp abrasives. Discard them as soon as they seem dull. This eats up the sandpaper, but it helps you control the temperature of the wood.

7

Finish the bowl. Finish the bowl *immediately* after turning it. This helps stabilize the moisture content of the wood, which in turn keeps it from splitting. You can apply most finishes while the bowl is still on the lathe. Simply dip a cloth pad into the finish and hold it against the revolving bowl. The rotation evenly distributes the finish and helps it to dry quickly.

TRY THIS! Rude Osolnik finishes his bowl with a mixture of tung oil and spar varnish — more oil than varnish. When applied to turnings on the lathe, a deep, semigloss finish builds up quickly. This finish requires almost no rub-out, just a light application of paste wax after it dries thoroughly.

8 **Remove the finished bowl from the faceplate.** Cut the bowl free of the faceplate with a parting tool. As you do this, avoid the screws that hold the turning to the faceplate. Also be careful not to cut through to the inside of the bowl or make the bottom too thin. The bottom should be ¼" to ½" thick, depending on the size of the finished bowl.

Sand the bottom of the bowl and apply a finish. If you wish, glue a piece a felt to the bottom after the finish dries.

Variations

Turning a Cup with a Handle

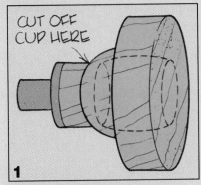

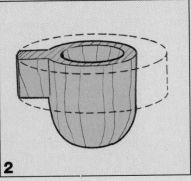

To make a cup with a handle, first turn just the **bottom** portion of the outside. Leave a wide, thick ring around the top. Then turn the inside of the cup.

Using a band saw, cut away as much stock as possible from the ring around the top. Leave enough stock on one side of the cup to form a handle.

Carve the finished shape of the handle. Also carve away any excess stock from the side of the cup that you couldn't remove with the band saw. Then finish sand the cup and handle.

Turning a Covered Container

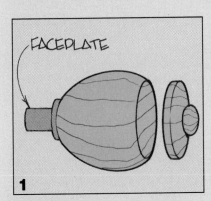

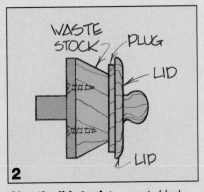

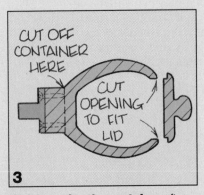

To make a jar or any other covered container, first rough-turn the outside shape of both the container and the lid. Using a parting tool, separate the lid from the container.

Glue the lid stock to a waste block, then mount the waste on a faceplate. Turn the lid shape, complete with a lip and a plug, as shown. Sand the lid and cut it free of the waste block.

Finish turning the container after you've completed the lid. Shape the outside, then the inside. At first, cut the opening at the top of the container too small for the lid. Carefully expand it until the lid fits properly. The opening should be wider than the plug, but smaller than the lip.

Shaker Peg Rail and Clothes Hangers

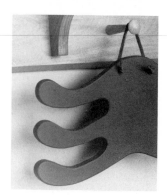

Although the Shakers did not invent the peg rail, they certainly invented many different uses for it. They developed an entire storage system around the simple peg, including shelves, cupboards, mirrors, plate racks, candle holders, even chairs that hung from the walls. One of their best-known inventions, still very much in use today, was the clothes hanger.

The wooden clothes hangers shown are copies of hangers made in the early nineteenth century at the Shaker community in South Union, Kentucky. They're just simple cutouts hung on a peg by a leather thong, but they exemplify many of the virtues of Shaker craftsmanship. The single hanger displays the grace and beauty the Shakers found in simplicity. It's pleasant to look at even when not in use. The triple hanger shows their dedication to utility. It held an entire suit — jacket, shirt, and trousers — on a single peg. (The trousers hung by their belt loops.)

The peg rail and shelf is not a direct copy of a Shaker original, but it borrows many elements from Shaker design. The piece is simple and utilitarian, with little ornament. It shows an economical use

of space and materials: The backboard supports both pegs and a shelf. The stock is thinner than

usual, although the construction remains strong. The chamfer around the edges makes the boards

seem thinner yet. This, in turn, gives the piece a delicate and graceful look.

Materials List

FINISHED DIMENSIONS

PARTS

Clothes Hangers

A. Single hanger   ½" x 3⅛" x 15"
B. Triple hanger   ½" x 6¾" x 12"

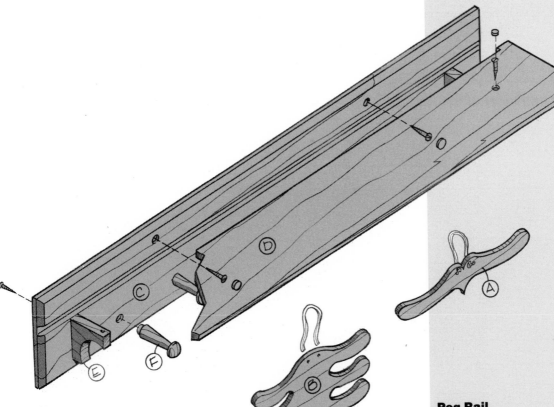

EXPLODED VIEW

Peg Rail

C. Backboard   ⅝" x 7½" x 46"
D. Shelf   ⅝" x 7½" x 48"
E. Braces (2)   ⅝" x 3¼" x 3¼"
F. Pegs (6)   ⅞" dia. x 3½"

HARDWARE

Clothes Hangers

Leather thongs (3"–4" per hanger)

Peg Rail

#8 x 1¼" Flathead wood screws (8)
#12 x 2½" Roundhead wood screws
  (1–2) *or:*
¼" Molly anchors and roundhead bolts
  (1–2)
½" Screw hole plugs (2)

Making the Clothes Hangers

1 **Select and prepare the stock.** Shaker craftsmen cut hangers from hard, strong materials which could be sanded to a glassy finish. They preferred maple, birch, and hickory. Woods such as pine and cedar were deemed too soft to be durable — although cedar keeps clothes sweet smelling and moth-free. Open-grained woods such as oak might splinter and snag the clothes.

Decide how many hangers you want to make. Select a suitable wood, then plane it to ½" thick. Cut the stock to size, making as many pieces as you need.

2 **Cut the hanger shapes.** Enlarge the *Hanger Patterns* and trace them on the stock. Cut the shapes on a band saw or scroll saw, then sand the edges to remove the saw marks.

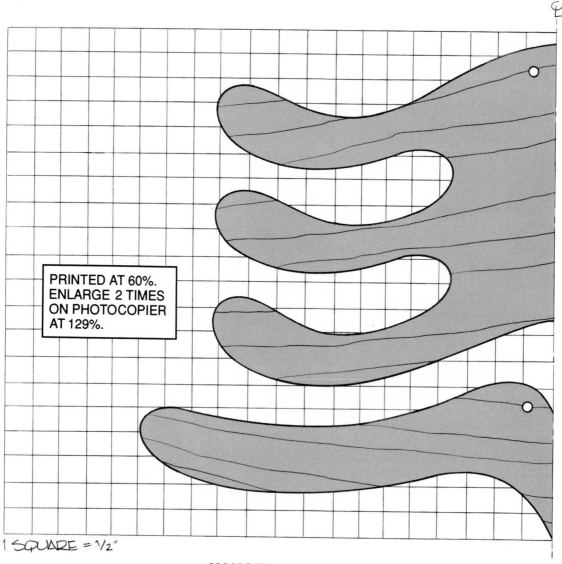

PRINTED AT 60%.
ENLARGE 2 TIMES
ON PHOTOCOPIER
AT 129%.

1 SQUARE = ½"

HANGER PATTERNS

TRY THIS!   If you're making more than one copy of a hanger, stack the workpieces and tape them together. Trace the pattern on the top workpiece, then cut the whole stack.

3 **Drill the holes for the thongs.**   Drill two $^3/_{16}$"-diameter holes in each hanger, near the top edge, as shown in the *Single Hanger Layout* and *Triple Hanger Layout*. If you're making several copies of a hanger, stack them up and drill them all at once.

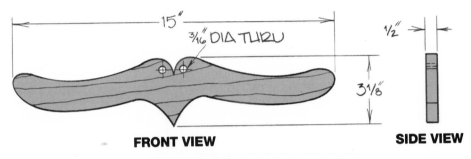

SINGLE HANGER LAYOUT

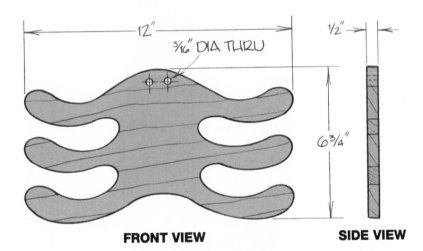

TRIPLE HANGER LAYOUT

4 **Sand and finish the hangers.**   Round the edges of each hanger with a file or sandpaper. Pay particular attention to the top edges. There should be no hard corners that can crease the clothes. Rounding the corners also lessens the chance of splinters and snags. Finish sand the hangers so they're glass smooth.

Apply a finish. The Shakers customarily painted their hangers with milk paint. You can use a commercial milk paint, latex paint, or acrylic paint to achieve the same effect. The hangers shown were painted with acrylic paint.

After the finish dries, insert a leather thong through the holes in each hanger. It should be just long enough to loop over a peg. Tie knots in the ends to keep it from pulling out of the holes.

Making the Peg Rail

1 ***Select the stock and cut it to size.*** Like the hangers, the pegs and rails usually were made from maple, birch, or hickory. The peg rail shown is birch. Most commercially available pegs are either birch or maple. You can purchase them from crafts stores and most mail-order woodworking suppliers.

Select an appropriate wood. Also decide how long you want to make the shelf — you can increase or decrease the length in 6" increments. If you're making your own pegs, cut 1" x 1" x 5" turning blocks. Plane the rest of the wood ⅝" thick, then cut the backboard, shelf, and braces to size.

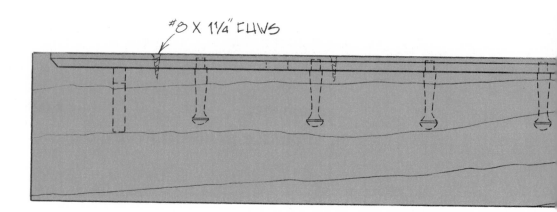

TOP VIEW

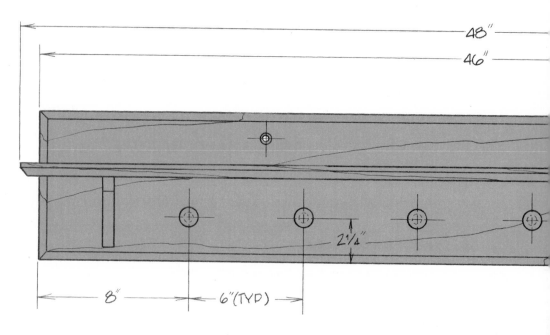

FRONT VIEW

2 ***Chamfer the backboard and shelf.*** Use
a table-mounted router and a piloted chamfering
bit to cut 45° chamfers in the backboard and shelf. (See
Figure 1.) Chamfer all four edges of the backboard, but
just the ends and front edge of the shelf. Leave the back
edge square.

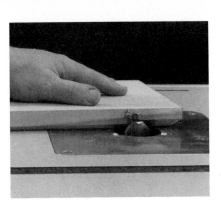

***1/**Rout the cham-
fers in several
passes, cutting just
⅛"–¼" deeper with
each pass. If you
try to cut a deep
chamfer in a single
pass, the wood
will burn.*

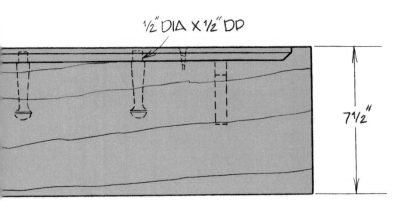

½" DIA X ½" DP

7½"

¼"

⅝"

45° CHAMFER

EDGE DETAIL

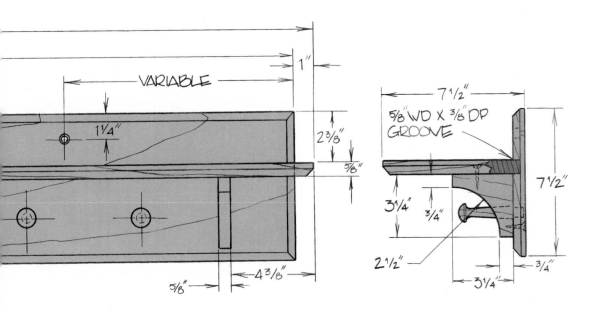

1"

VARIABLE

1¼"

2⅜"

⅝"

5⁄8" ⟵

4⅜"

7½"

⅝ WD X ⅜ DP
GROOVE

7½"

3¼"   ¾"

2½"

3¼"

¾"

SIDE VIEW

3 **Cut the joinery.** Cut a ⅝"-wide, ⅜"-deep groove in the backboard, as shown in the *Front View* and *Side View*. You can make this joint with either a dado cutter or a table-mounted router. If you use a router, cut the groove in several passes with a ½"-diameter straight bit. Cut a ½"-wide groove first, guiding the workpiece with a fence or straightedge. Move the fence ⅛" away from the bit and widen the groove to ⅝".

Cut a ¼"-deep, 46"-long notch, centered in the back edge of the shelf, as shown in the *Notch Detail*. Don't worry if the long edge of the notch isn't perfectly straight or smooth. A rough, wandering cut will be hidden when you assemble the peg rail — as long as it isn't too rough and doesn't wander more than ¹⁄₁₆" or so.

Drill the ½"-diameter, ½"-deep round mortises in the peg rail, as shown in the *Front View*. If you use a brad-point bit, the brad may poke through the back face. This is okay, and even useful: Excess glue can escape from the hole when you assemble the peg rail.

Determine the positions of the holes you need to hang the peg rail. If possible, center the holes over

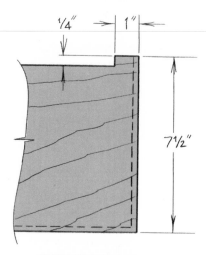

NOTCH DETAIL

studs in the wall. Mark the locations near the top edge of the backboard. From the front, bore ½"-diameter, ¼"-deep holes at each mark. Then drill ¼"-diameter holes in the center of these larger holes through to the other side.

4 **Cut the braces.** With a compass, mark the arch of the brace on one piece. Place the marked piece on top of the other, and tape them together. Cut both pieces at once, using a band saw or scroll saw. Remove the tape and sand the sawed edges.

5 **Turn the pegs.** If you want to turn your own pegs, trace the *Peg Profile* on a ¼" plywood scrap and cut a template. As you turn each peg, compare the shape to the template and try to match the contours. (See Figure 2.) Use calipers to ensure that the tenon on the end of the peg is precisely ½" in diameter. Finish sand the pegs on the lathe.

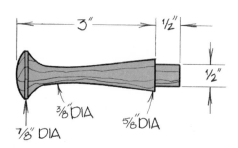

PEG PROFILE

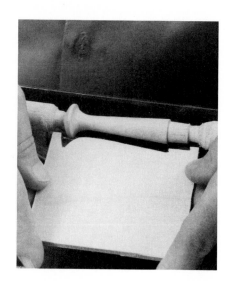

*2/Compare the shape of each peg to a template as you turn it. This will ensure that all the pegs are similar. Don't worry if they aren't **precisely** the same. The shapes aren't critical, as long as they're close.*

6 **Assemble and finish the peg rail.** Finish sand the backboard, shelf, and braces. Glue the shelf in the backboard groove. Reinforce the joint by driving screws through the back of the backboard and into the shelf. Countersink the screws.

Glue the braces to the backboard and the shelf, and reinforce them with screws. Countersink the screws that you drive through the backboard, and counterbore *and* countersink the screws that you drive through the shelf. Glue wooden plugs in the counterbores to hide the screw heads.

Glue the pegs in the round mortises. When the glue dries, do the necessary touch-up sanding and apply a finish.

7 **Hang the peg rail.** Attach the peg rail to a wall, using the holes in the backboard. If there is a stud behind a hole, drive a #12 x 2½" roundhead wood screw through the backboard and into the stud. If there is no stud, install a ¼" molly anchor in the wall behind the hole. Drive a ¼" roundhead bolt into the anchor. Cover the heads of the screws or bolts with wooden screw hole buttons. Paint or finish the heads of the buttons to match the peg rail.

Drill Press Turning Jig

If you don't have a lathe, you can make small turnings on a drill press with this simple jig. Fashion the wooden parts from scraps of hardwood, such as maple or birch. Cut the head off a ¼"-diameter carriage bolt and grind a point on one end to make the metal pivot. Clamp the jig to the worktable of the drill press so the pivot is directly beneath the chuck.

1

Clamp the top end of the stock in the chuck, and rest the bottom end on the pivot. If the diameter of the stock is too large to hold in the chuck, drive a #12 x 1 ¼" screw into the top end, leaving the shank exposed. Cut the head off the screw and clamp the shank in the chuck.

2

Set the drill press to run at a low speed and turn it on. Cut the shape of the turning with chisels, using the vertical member of the jig as a tool rest. Oil the pivot now and then to keep the lower portion of the stock from burning or wearing away. When you have completed the turning, remove it from the jig and cut away the waste.

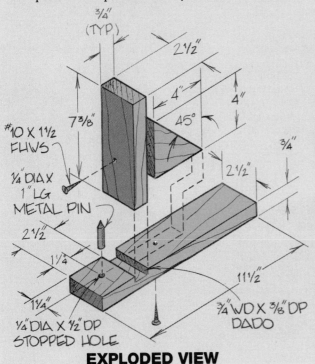

¾"
(TYP)

2½"

4"

4"

45°

7⅜"

#10 X 1½
FHWS

¼ DIA X
1" LG
METAL PIN

2½"

¾"

2½"

11½"

1¼"

1¼"

¾" WD X ⅜" DP
DADO

¼" DIA X ½" DP
STOPPED HOLE

EXPLODED VIEW

Bird Decoys

During the eighteenth and nineteenth centuries, feathers were in high fashion. Inhabitants of rural and coastal areas often supplemented their income by catching birds and selling the plumage to haberdashers and dressmakers. Not only did they hunt large game birds, like pheasant and ducks, but they also snared many small, colorful songbirds and shore birds — bluebirds, woodpeckers, goldfinches, plovers, wimbrels, and so on. When times were especially bad, they ate them, too. After plucking the feathers, the hunters boiled the small bird carcasses, removed the meat, and baked it in a "peep pie."

Bird hunters used simple decoys like those shown to attract their prey. Because of their social and territorial instincts, birds will often investigate anything that's shaped and colored like another member of their species. So the hunters made wooden cutouts, painted them, and mounted them on sticks.

Decoys weren't just used by hunters. Some folks set them out to attract songbirds; others decorated their yards and garden with them. Still others mounted the decoys on bases and set them on a bookshelf or mantle. Indoors or out, the wooden birds added a bit of color and fancy to their homes.

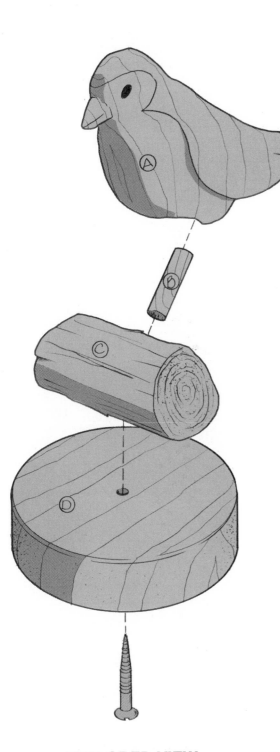

EXPLODED VIEW

Materials List
FINISHED DIMENSIONS

PARTS

Scarlet Tanager
A.	Body	¾" x 2" x 7"
B.	Leg dowel	¼" dia. x 1½"
C.	Perch	1" dia.* x 2½"*
D.	Base	3" dia. x ½"

Goldfinch
A.	Body	¾" x 1¾" x 4⅞"
B.	Leg dowel	³⁄₁₆" x 1"
C.	Perch	¾" dia.* x 2"*
D.	Base	2½" dia. x ½"

White-Breasted Nuthatch
A.	Body	¾" x 2½" x 5"
B.	Leg dowel	³⁄₁₆" dia. x 1"
C.	Perch	1" dia.* x 5"*
D.	Base	3" dia. x ½"

Wilson's Warbler
A.	Body	¾" x 1⅝" x 4"
B.	Leg dowel	³⁄₁₆" x 1"
C.	Perch	¾" dia.* x 3"*
D.	Base	2½" dia. x ½"

Eastern Bluebird
A.	Body	¾" x 2" x 6¼"
B.	Leg dowel	¼" dia. x 1½"
C.	Perch	1" dia.* x 2½"*
D.	Base	3" dia. x ½"

Red-Bellied Woodpecker
A.	Body	¾" x 3" x 8⅛"
B.	Leg dowel	¼" dia. x 1½"
C.	Perch	1½" dia.* x 9"*
D.	Base	3½" dia. x ½"

*Since the perches are made from
actual limbs and branches, the measurements are approximate.*

HARDWARE

#8 x 1¼" Flathead wood screws
  (1 per decoy)

1

Select and prepare the stock. Since you'll be painting each decoy's body, leg dowel, and base, you should make the parts from durable, light-colored wood. The stock for the body should also be easy to carve, if you want to sculpt the features. Basswood is the best choice for the body, followed by butternut and lauan mahogany. (For more information on choosing woods for carving, see the introductory chapter, Chust for So.) Use commercial dowel stock for the leg dowel, and an inexpensive near-white wood for the base. Poplar, pine, maple, and birch will all work well.

For the perch, find a small, dry branch from any nearby tree. If you don't own any trees with dead limbs, go for a walk in a park or a forest. Worm-eaten deadfalls make especially interesting perches.

After choosing the stock, plane the flat pieces to the thicknesses needed — ¾" for the body, ½" for the base. Cut all the parts to size.

2

Cut the body and the base. Transfer the outside pattern line and the location of the leg dowel hole to the body stock. Or: Photocopy the pattern and stick it to the stock with spray adhesive. Use a compass to scribe a circle (of the diameter specified in the Materials List) on the base stock. Cut the body shape and the base on a band saw or scroll saw, then sand the sawed edges.

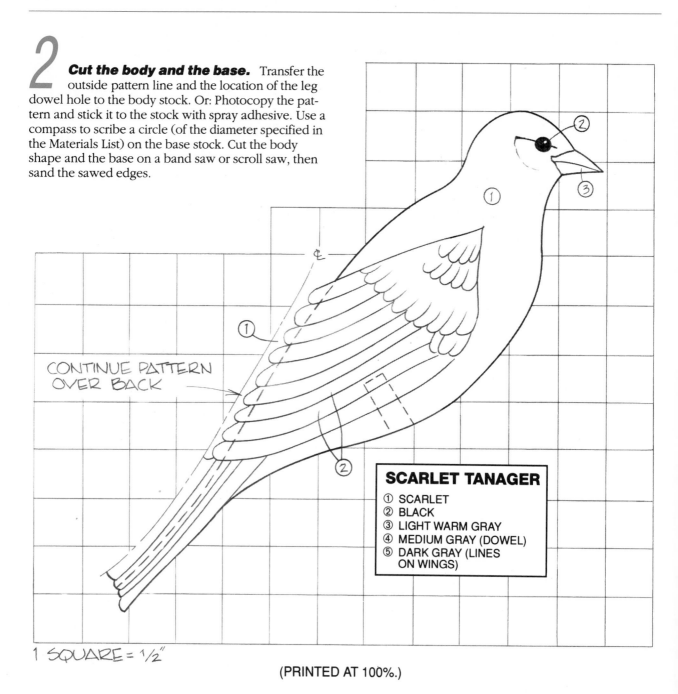

CONTINUE PATTERN OVER BACK

SCARLET TANAGER
① SCARLET
② BLACK
③ LIGHT WARM GRAY
④ MEDIUM GRAY (DOWEL)
⑤ DARK GRAY (LINES ON WINGS)

1 SQUARE = ½"

(PRINTED AT 100%.)

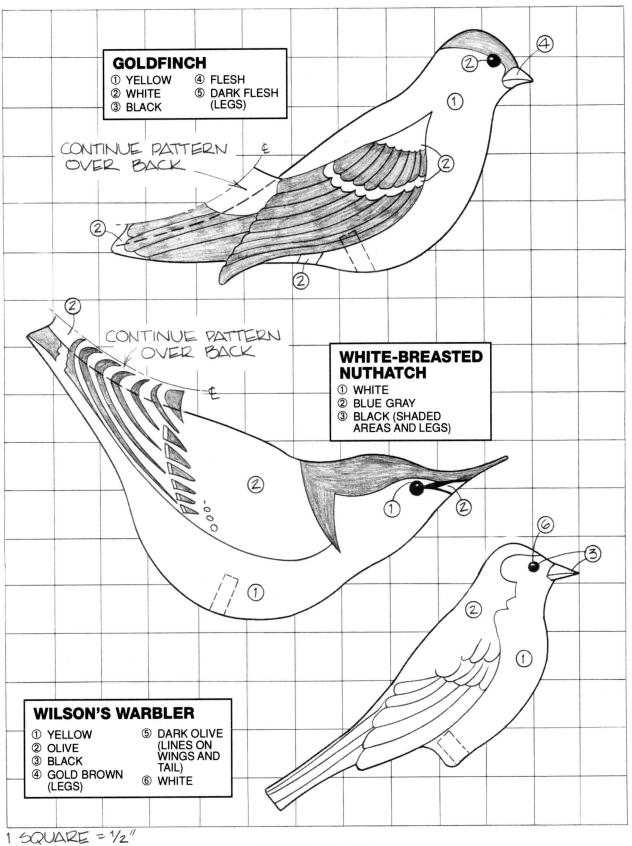

GOLDFINCH
① YELLOW ④ FLESH
② WHITE ⑤ DARK FLESH
③ BLACK (LEGS)

CONTINUE PATTERN OVER BACK

CONTINUE PATTERN OVER BACK

WHITE-BREASTED NUTHATCH
① WHITE
② BLUE GRAY
③ BLACK (SHADED AREAS AND LEGS)

WILSON'S WARBLER
① YELLOW ⑤ DARK OLIVE
② OLIVE (LINES ON
③ BLACK WINGS AND
④ GOLD BROWN TAIL)
(LEGS) ⑥ WHITE

1 SQUARE = ½"

(PRINTED AT 100%.)

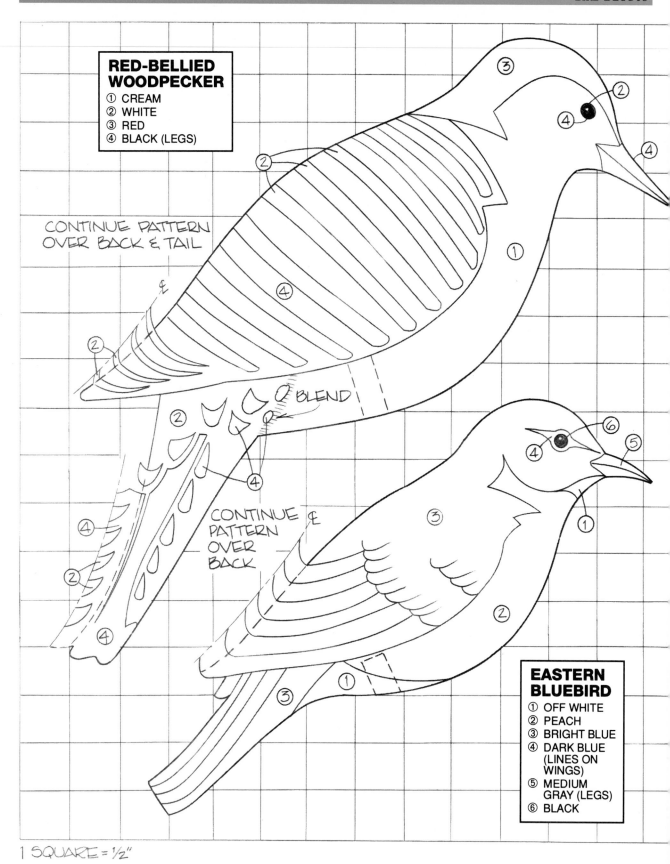

RED-BELLIED WOODPECKER
① CREAM
② WHITE
③ RED
④ BLACK (LEGS)

CONTINUE PATTERN OVER BACK & TAIL

BLEND

CONTINUE PATTERN OVER BACK

EASTERN BLUEBIRD
① OFF WHITE
② PEACH
③ BRIGHT BLUE
④ DARK BLUE (LINES ON WINGS)
⑤ MEDIUM GRAY (LEGS)
⑥ BLACK

1 SQUARE = ½"

(PRINTED AT 100%.)

3 *Drill the leg dowel hole in the body.*

Clamp the body flat on your workbench. Mount the appropriate bit in a hand-held power drill, then line it up with the leg hole marks on the pattern. Center the bit between the left and right sides of the body. Bore the leg hole ⅜"–½" deep. (See Figure 1.)

Note: The depth of the leg hole in the body (and later, in the perch) determines how much of the leg owel will show on the assembled decoy. Since birds usually tuck their legs under them when they perch, not much will be exposed — just ¼" (on the smaller birds) to ½" (on the larger ones). If you aren't sure how deep to drill a hole, consult a birdwatcher's guide book for photos and drawings of the pertinent species.

1/Line up the drill bit with the pattern marks and bore the hole for the leg dowel. Wrap a piece of tape around the bit to help gauge the depth of the hole.

4 *Carve the body.* Using a carving knife,

round over the edges of the body to make the shape more realistic. If you wish, you can also carve some features. Taper the thickness of the neck, to make the head slightly narrower than the rest of the body. Do the same to the beak, to make it narrower than the head. Cut away stock just underneath the wings, so they seem to stand out slightly from the body. (See Figure 2.) When you've finished carving, sand the body to remove any knife marks.

2/To make the wings stand out from the body, first score each wing along the lower edge, as shown. Then pare away stock from the belly just beneath the wing, until the wing is 1/16"–⅛" higher than the belly.

5 *Assemble the decoy.* Strip the bark from

the perch. Decide where you want to mount the body, and estimate the angle of the hole. Drill the hole ⅜"–½" deep, the same depth as the hole in the body.

Temporarily mount the bird on the leg dowel and insert the leg dowel in the perch. Hold the assembly so the body is at a realistic angle — the position that you'd expect to see the bird when it's perched. Then sand a flat on the bottom of the perch. When the assembly is mounted to the base, this flat will hold the decoy at the proper angle.

Note: Different bird species perch in different positions. For example, the nuthatch often hangs upside down on the side of a tree. A woodpecker clings right side up, but braces itself with its tail. If you are unsure as to how to position a bird on a perch, consult the illustrations in a birdwatcher's guide book.

Take apart the body, leg dowel, and perch. Round the upper edge of the base with a file, then finish sand all the parts. Glue the perch to the base. To reinforce it, drive a flathead wood screw up through the base and into the flat area of the perch.

6 *Paint the decoy.* Draw the interior pattern

lines on the body. Color the body, leg dowel, and base with latex or acrylic paint. Follow the color codes on the drawings, or refer to a birdwatcher's guide book for help in choosing the correct colors. After the paint dries, glue one end of the leg dowel in the body and the other in the perch.

Toy Wagon

Child's play is often an imitation of grown-up work. The toy wagon is a good example. Since much of the farm work in nineteenth-century America was accomplished with a wagon, rural children coveted child-sized models so they could imitate their parents.

These toy wagons came in all shapes and sizes, some handmade, others manufactured by toy companies. Some were miniature copies of the real thing, with spoked wheels and metal springs. Most were much simpler — just a wooden box on four wooden wheels. A few could be hitched to a trained goat, but most were designed to be pulled by hand.

The wagon shown is typical of many that parents once made for toddlers. The box is just large enough to hold a stuffed animal or a set of blocks. The construction is light, to make the wagon easy to pull, and the wheels are set wide to prevent the wagon from overturning. Most of the parts are wooden; you can purchase the few metal parts in any hardware store.

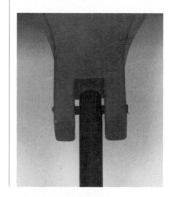

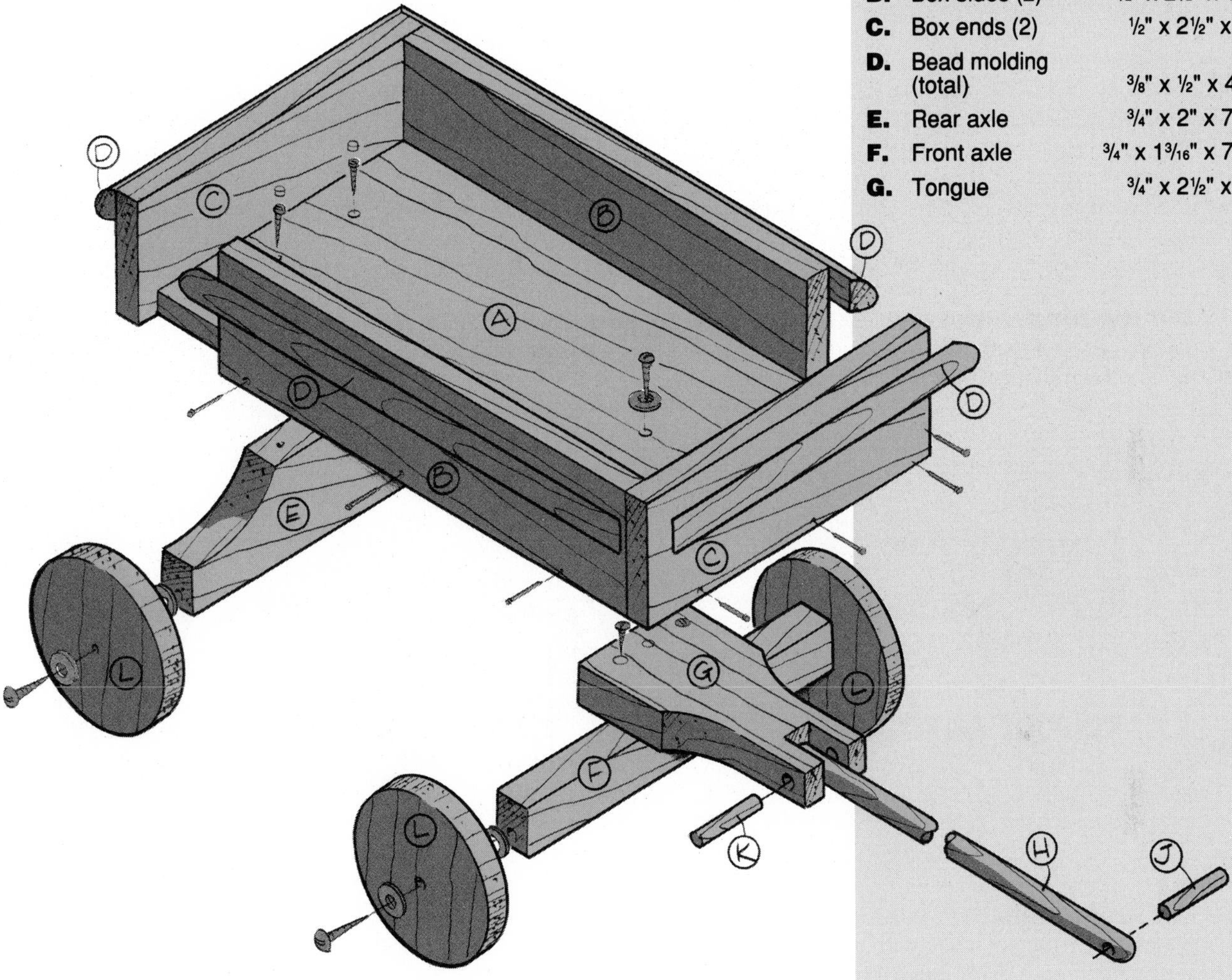

Materials List

PARTS

A.	Box bottom	½" x 6" x 11"
B.	Box sides (2)	½" x 2½" x 11"
C.	Box ends (2)	½" x 2½" x 7"
D.	Bead molding (total)	⅜" x ½" x 40"
E.	Rear axle	¾" x 2" x 7½"
F.	Front axle	¾" x 1³⁄₁₆" x 7½"
G.	Tongue	¾" x 2½" x 5"

EXPLODED VIEW

H.	Handle	½" dia. x 10¾"
J.	Crossbar	¼" dia. x 3"
K.	Pin	³⁄₁₆" dia. x 1½"
L.	Wheels (4)	3¼" dia. x ¾"

HARDWARE

#12 x 1½" Roundhead wood screws (5)
#12 Flat washers (10)
#8 x 1¼" Flathead wood screws (4)
1" Wire brads (12–20)
⅜"-diameter Wooden plugs (2)

1 Select the stock and cut it to size.

Toy wagons were usually made from whatever lumber was on hand. Craftsmen often used white pine for the box and other nonmoving parts, because it was so easy to work. They made the wheels and handle from harder woods, such as maple and birch, to stand up to constant use — and abuse.

There are, however, no traditional choices. You can make your wagon from any domestic wood. Fashion the wheels from a hard, durable wood; the handle, crossbar, and pin from commercial dowel stock; and the other parts from whatever scraps are lying around.

If you have some ½" plywood, use it for the bottom of the box. Even though plywood wasn't available to old-time craftsmen, it's a good choice. A bottom made of solid wood will expand and contract with changes in the weather, stressing the corner joints of the box. Plywood is relatively stable and will not break the joints.

After you select the wood, plane the thicknesses you need — ½" for the box parts, molding, and wheels; and ¾" for the axles and tongue. Cut all the parts to the sizes you need *except* the bead molding. You'll make this later.

2 Cut the tongue and rear axle.

Lay out the shapes of the tongue and the rear axle on the stock, as shown in the *Tongue Layout* and *Rear Axle Layout*. Cut the shapes with a band saw, scroll saw, or saber saw, then sand the sawed edges.

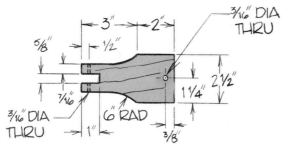

TONGUE LAYOUT

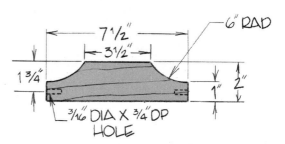

REAR AXLE LAYOUT

3 Cut the wheels.

Draw four 3¼"-diameter circles on the wheel stock with a compass, and mark the exact center of each. Cut each wheel, then drill a ¼"-diameter hole through the center.

If you have a stationary disk sander, belt sander, or strip sander, you can use it to make perfectly round wheels. Follow this procedure:

Cut each wheel a little wide of the circumference. Make a simple sanding jig, as shown in the *Wheel Sanding Jig* drawing. Place a wheel on the dowel pivot and clamp this jig to the worktable of the sander. The wheel should just touch the sanding surface. Turn the sander on, loosen a clamp, and slowly advance the jig until you have sanded up to the circumference line. (See Figure 1.)

Tighten the clamp, then slowly turn the wheel around the pivot. (See Figure 2.) The sander will grind the wheel just up to the circumference line, making a wheel exactly 3¼" in diameter. Do this for the other three wheels.

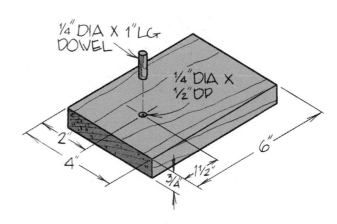

WHEEL-SANDING JIG

1/To sand a wheel to a precise diameter, cut it a little large. Fit it over the pivot of a sanding jig, then sand up to the circumference line.

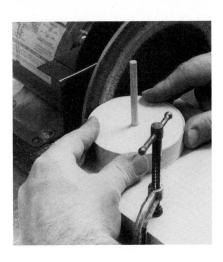

2/With the sander running, turn the wheel around the pivot. The sander will grind away stock just up to the circumference line. If you use a disk sander, be sure to work on the "down" side of the disk, so the rotation holds the wheel on the pivot.

---

4 **Drill the axle and pivot holes.** Using a drill press, bore ³/₁₆"-diameter, ¾"-deep axle holes in the ends of the front and rear axles. (See Figure 3.) These holes should be ¼" from the bottom edge of the axle stock.

3/To bore holes in the ends of the axles, clamp them vertically in a wood screw. Use a square to check that the pieces are straight up and down. Then, using the wood screw as a stand, bore a hole in each end of each axle.

After making the axle holes, drill the others you need:
- A ¼"-diameter pivot hole in the box bottom, as shown in the *Side View*
- A ¼"-diameter hole through the handle, near the front end, to hold the crossbar
- A ³/₁₆"-diameter pilot hole in the tongue, as shown in the *Tongue Layout,* to attach the tongue to the box
- A ³/₁₆"-diameter hole through the forks of the tongue to pin the handle to the tongue
- A ³/₁₆"-diameter hole near the rear end of the handle, to fit the pin

TRY THIS! A V-jig will keep the handle steady as you drill it. To make this jig, cut a V-shaped groove in a scrap of wood. Place the handle in the groove.

TRY THIS! The holes at either end of the handle must line up, so the pin and the crossbar will be parallel to each other. To align them properly, place the handle in a shallow groove. (The groove between the parts of a door casing will do.) Using the edge of this groove as a straightedge, mark a line down the side of the handle. Place the handle on your drill press with the line facing up, then drill the holes through the line.

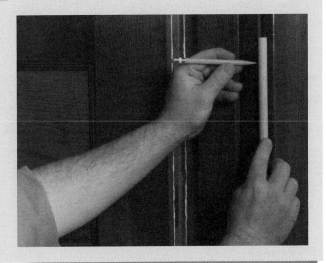

5 **Make the bead molding.** Select a scrap of ½"-thick stock, at least 3" wide and 20" long. Using a table-mounted router and a ¼" quarter-round bit, round over both edges of the stock, as shown in the *Molding Profile*. This will form a bead on the edges of the stock. Rip both beads free on a table saw, making at least 40" of bead molding. (See Figure 4.)

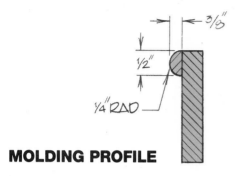

MOLDING PROFILE

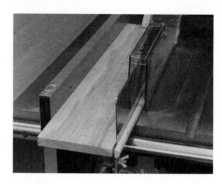

4/When making small, slender moldings, **always** shape the edge of a wider board first, then rip the shape from the board. Never try to shape narrow stock; it may come apart in your hands.

6 **Assemble the box.** Finish sand all the wagon parts. Glue the box bottom, sides, and ends together, reinforcing the joints with brads. Let the glue dry, then sand the joints clean and flush.

Cut the bead molding to fit around the perimeter of the box, mitering the ends. Glue the molding to the box, flush with the upper edges. After the glue dries, sand the molding, rounding the corners.

7 **Assemble and attach the axles.** Glue the front axle to the tongue, and the rear axle to the underside of the box. Reinforce the glue joints with flathead wood screws. Counterbore *and* countersink the screws that hold the rear axle to the box, then cover the heads with wooden plugs. Just countersink the screws that hold the tongue to the front axle. There's no need to hide the heads; you won't see them when the wagon is assembled.

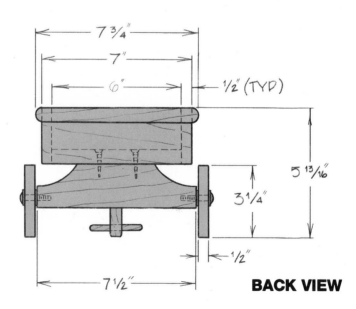

BACK VIEW

After the glue dries, sand the front axle assembly clean and flush. Put a washer over a roundhead screw, insert it in the pivot hole in the box bottom, and put another washer over the end of the screw. (When correctly assembled, there should be a washer between the screw head and the box bottom, and another between the box bottom and the tongue.) Drive the screw into the pilot hole in the tongue. Tighten it so the tongue is snug, but loose enough to pivot freely.

8 **Attach the wheels.** Install the wheels on the axles in much the same manner that you attached the front axle assembly to the box. Drive screws through the wheels and into the axles, with a washer on either side of the wheels. These washers keep the wheels from rubbing the axles and the screw heads.

Note: If the wagon doesn't sit solidly on a flat surface, one wheel may be slightly larger than the other three. Determine which wheel is too big, then sand it slightly smaller on the wheel sanding jig.

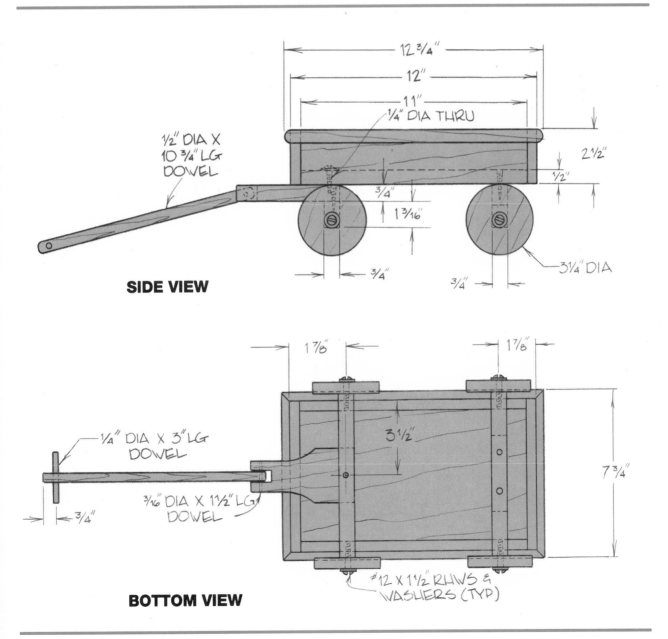

9 Assemble and attach the handle.
Glue the crossbar in the ¼"-diameter hole in one end of the handle. Place the other end of the handle between the forks of the tongue. Insert the pin through the ³⁄₁₆"-diameter holes in both parts to keep the handle in place. Glue the pin in the tongue, but *not* in the handle. The handle should move up and down freely.

TRY THIS! To keep the handle from sticking to the pin, wax the *middle* section of the pin. Be careful not to get any wax on the ends, where you want to glue the pin in the tongue.

10 Finish the wagon.
Remove the wheels from the axles, and the front axle/handle assembly from the box. Do any necessary touch-up sanding, then paint the wagon. Follow the patterns shown, or invent your own.

To make the wagon look old, lightly sand the edges to remove some of the paint. This will simulate normal wear and tear on the finish. Then apply a thin coat of *tinted* shellac over the paint. Tint the shellac with burnt umber artist's oil paint to dull the color of the finish and make it look old. (Artist's oils can be purchased at most paint stores and arts-and-crafts stores.) You can also use brown aniline dye as a tint.

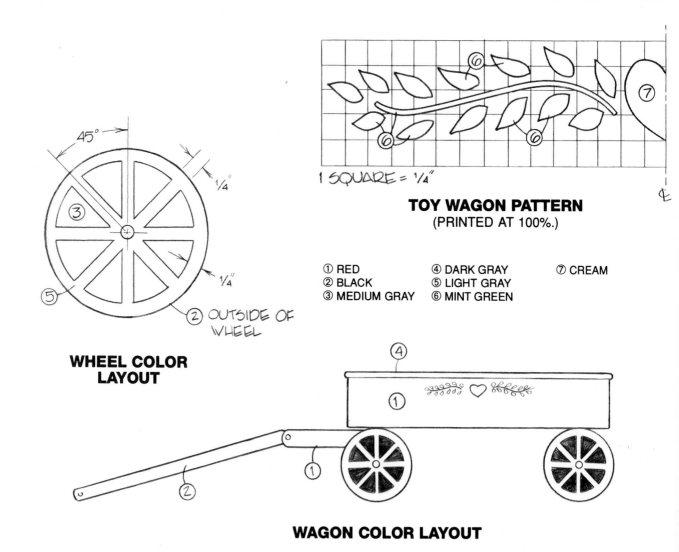

1 SQUARE = ¼"

TOY WAGON PATTERN
(PRINTED AT 100%.)

① RED   ④ DARK GRAY   ⑦ CREAM
② BLACK   ⑤ LIGHT GRAY
③ MEDIUM GRAY   ⑥ MINT GREEN

WHEEL COLOR LAYOUT

WAGON COLOR LAYOUT

Shaker Oval Boxes

The country folk in both Europe and America used oval-shaped bentwood boxes for many purposes. Usually, they stored small household items in them. But sometimes a country handyman would add a handle to a box to use it for gathering and carrying. Old labels and business records show that these boxes were occasionally employed as packages and shipping containers. Some were lined with fabric to make sewing boxes; still others were filled with wood shavings to serve as spittoons.

Whatever their use, many folks preferred them over other boxes for their economy, durability, and design. A bentwood box has very thin sides and no corner joints. Because of this, it requires fewer materials and less time to craft than a box with corners. The oval shape makes the box deceptively strong; the elliptical curve keeps the thin sides from collapsing, even during rough use. The flat side of the ellipse provides a good location for joinery. The distinctive swallowtail joints allow the parts of the box to expand and contract without distorting or causing the lid to bind. Finally, the oval shape fits the hand comfortably and is easy to grasp.

Of the many country craftsmen who built oval boxes, perhaps the best remembered are the United Society of Believers in Christ's Second Appearing — the Shakers. They refined the form, making oval boxes that were lighter, better fitting, and more uniform than those of most box makers. Several Shaker communities manufactured these boxes "by the numbers," making seven graduated sizes from #0 (the smallest) to #6 (the largest). The boxes fit or "nested" inside one another, saving storage space when not in use. A set of seven Shaker oval boxes — one of each size — was known as a nest of boxes.

The Shakers still manufacture oval boxes today at Sabbathday Lake, Maine — the last remaining active Shaker community. And many contemporary craftsmen and craftswomen continue to make boxes in the Shaker tradition. The nest of boxes shown was made by Larry Owrey of Franklin, Ohio. Larry, a high school social studies teacher, demonstrates box making at the site of the old South Union Shaker Community near Bowling Green, Kentucky. He also conducts seminars around the Midwest.

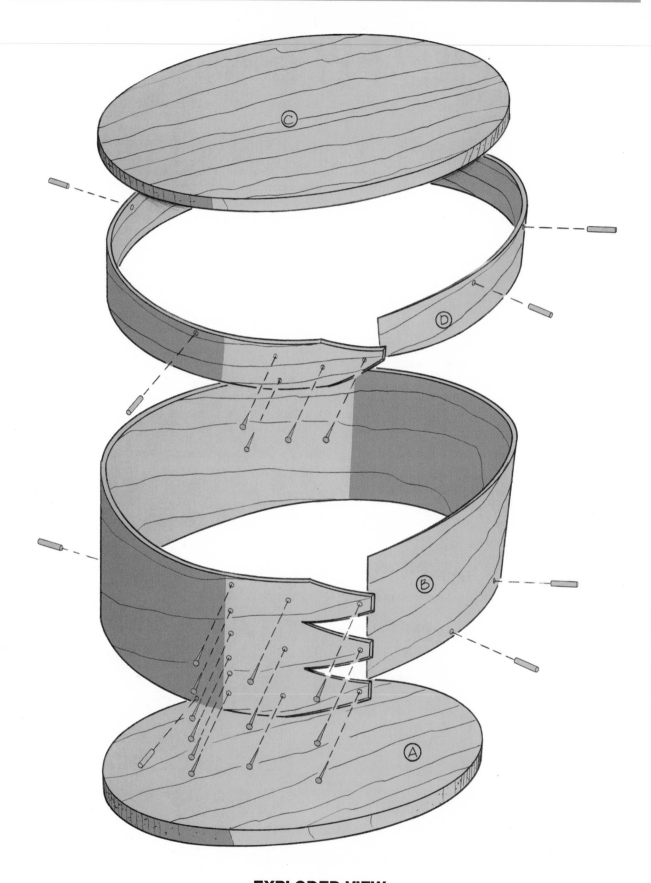

EXPLODED VIEW

Materials List

FINISHED DIMENSIONS

PARTS

#0 Oval Box
A. Bottom   1/4" x 2" x 3⅝"
B. Side band   1/16" x 1 1/16" x 11½"
C. Lid   1/4" x 2⅛" x 3¾"
D. Lid band   1/16" x 7/16" x 12"

#1 Oval Box
A. Bottom   1/4" x 2 9/16" x 4 9/16"
B. Side band   1/16" x 1½" x 15½"
C. Lid   1/4" x 2 11/16" x 4 11/16"
D. Lid band   1/16" x ½" x 16"

#2 Oval Box
A. Bottom   1/4" x 3½" x 5¾"
B. Side band   1/16" x 2" x 19"
C. Lid   1/4" x 3⅝" x 5⅞"
D. Lid band   1/16" x ⅝" x 19¾"

#3 Oval Box
A. Bottom   1/4" x 4½" x 7"
B. Side band   3/32" x 2½" x 23"
C. Lid   1/4" x 4 11/16" x 7 3/16"
D. Lid band   3/32" x ¾" x 24"

#4 Oval Box
A. Bottom   1/4" x 5½" x 8¼"
B. Side band   3/32" x 3" x 26½"
C. Lid   1/4" x 5 11/16" x 8 7/16"
D. Lid band   3/32" x ¾" x 27½"

#5 Oval Box
A. Bottom   1/4" x 6½" x 9½"
B. Side band   3/32" x 3¾" x 31"
C. Lid   1/4" x 6 11/16" x 9 11/16"
D. Lid band   3/32" x ⅞" x 32"

#6 Oval Box
A. Bottom   1/4" x 7½" x 10¾"
B. Side band   3/32" x 4½" x 35¾"
C. Lid   1/4" x 7 11/16" x 10 15/16"
D. Lid band   3/32" x 1" x 37"

HARDWARE

#0 Oval Box
#1 Copper tacks (11)

#1 Oval Box
#1 Copper tacks (12)

2 Oval Box
#1½ Copper tacks (12)

#3 Oval Box
#1½ Copper tacks (12)

#4 Oval Box
#1½ Copper tacks (16)

#5 Oval Box
#2 Copper tacks (16)

#6 Oval Box
#2 Copper tacks (16)

Note: *You can purchase these tacks from the W.W. Cross Nail Company, P.O. Box 365, Jeffery, NH 03452.*

---

1 **Make the jigs.** Before you can make oval boxes, you need several special jigs: a poacher, box molds, dryers, and an anvil.

Poacher— This is a long, watertight trough in which you heat and soak the bands in hot water. Soaking makes them limber enough to bend. Larry brazed together sheets of copper to make his poacher; however, you don't have to go to this trouble or expense.

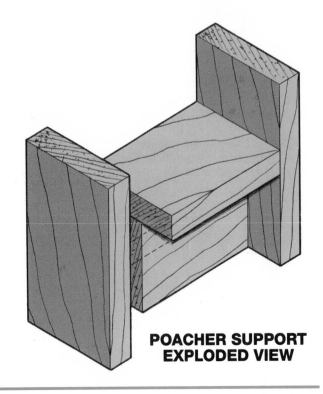

POACHER SUPPORT EXPLODED VIEW

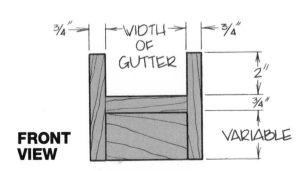

FRONT VIEW

1/Make a poacher from a length of galvanized gutter and two end caps. Support the gutter at both ends to keep it from sagging.

2/Cut the dryers wide of the line, then bevel sand the edges up to the lines. The beveled edge acts like a plug, wedging the dryer in an assembled side band. As the band cools and dries, the wood fibers harden, taking on the oval shape of the dryer.

Cut a piece of galvanized gutter about 40" long — slightly longer than the bands for the largest (#6) box. Cap the ends and seal them with a heat-resistant epoxy putty. (You don't need to solder the ends in place, as long as you heat the trough in the *middle* and don't get it hot enough to boil the water.) Set the trough on an electric hot plate, camp stove, or other compact heat source. If necessary, make wooden cradles for the ends to hold the trough upright and keep it from sagging. (See Figure 1.)

Box molds — The molds are thick, oval-shaped blocks, used to bend the sides immediately after they are poached. Make seven of them, one for each box size, from scrap wood. Plane each mold a little thicker than the width of the corresponding side band. For example, plane the block for the #1 box about 1¾" thick, since the side is 1½" wide. Cut the blocks to the same oval shapes as the *bottoms* of the boxes, shown in the *Lid/Bottom Patterns.*

each box. Cut ¾"-thick scrap to the same oval shapes as the *lids* of the boxes. (This shape is also shown in the *Lid/Bottom Patterns.*) Saw each dryer ¹⁄₁₆"–⅛" wide of the line, making it slightly larger than needed. Then sand up to the line with a stationary disk sander or belt sander. Tilt the sander's worktable 100° from the sanding surface. As you sand, you'll bevel the edge of the dryer at 10°, as shown in the *Dryer Edge Profile.* (See Figure 2.)

Drill one or two ¾"-diameter finger holes through each dryer. As a band cools and dries, it shrinks and tightens around the dryers. The holes will help you pull the dryers loose.

Anvil — You need an anvil to "clinch" or bend over the tacks on the inside of the bands. If you don't have one, make your own anvil from a length of 1½" O.D. iron pipe. Mount the pipe in a wooden framework, so it protrudes 6" from one end. To use the anvil, clamp it to your workbench with the pipe sticking out over the edge.

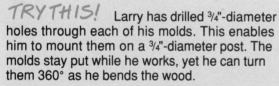

TRYTHIS! Larry has drilled ¾"-diameter holes through each of his molds. This enables him to mount them on a ¾"-diameter post. The molds stay put while he works, yet he can turn them 360° as he bends the wood.

Dryers — These are oval-shaped plugs with beveled edges. They set the shape of the box after you join the bands, as the poached wood dries. Make two dryers for

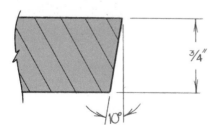

DRYER EDGE PROFILE

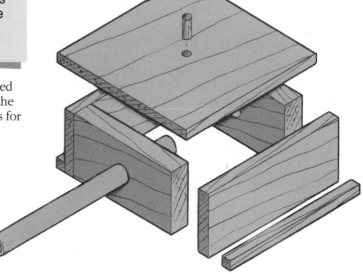

**ANVIL
EXPLODED VIEW**

TRY THIS! If you make an anvil, add a flat work surface to the top, as Larry did. In the center of this work surface, drill a ¾"-diameter, ½"-deep hole. Glue a ¾"-diameter, 1½" long dowel in the hole, and use it as a post to mount the molds. Then you can bend the bands and fasten them together on the same jig.

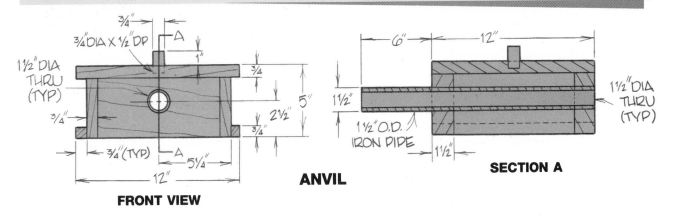

ANVIL

FRONT VIEW

SECTION A

2 Select the stock.

Traditionally, Shakers made the side and lid bands of oval boxes from hard maple, and the lids and bottoms from white pine. The hard maple strengthened the thin sides; pine lids and bottoms were easy to shape. Pine is also fairly durable, even though it's a soft wood.

The color of the wood was also important to the Shakers, since they usually painted the boxes. Both maple and pine are nearly white. Paint covers light-colored woods easily, and the colors remain vivid.

However, you can make oval boxes from almost any domestic wood. Larry makes a few from traditional maple and pine, but he mostly uses cherry and walnut. Fruitwoods, ash, poplar, birch, and hickory work well, too. Cedar makes good bottoms and lids, especially if you want to store cloth goods or foodstuffs in the boxes. Avoid brittle woods like redwood, or woods that splinter easily, like oak. Also avoid imported woods like mahogany; these aren't traditional.

3 Cut the band stock.

The bands must be very thin — just ¹⁄₁₆" for the two smaller boxes and ³⁄₃₂" for the other five. To make this thin stock, first cut the wood to the required band width. Then resaw it on a table saw or a band saw.

Use a table saw to slice the band stock for #0 through #4 boxes. Most 10" table saws have a 3" depth of cut — just deep enough to resaw the #4 bands. Cut the stock with a hollow-ground planer blade or a thin-kerf carbide-tipped blade. Both of these blades leave a very smooth surface: You won't have to do much sanding. To keep the thin stock from falling between the blade and the worktable, mount an insert in the table saw that reduces the open space around the blade. (See Figure 3.) If you don't have such an insert, you can make one. See Step-by-Step: Making a Table Saw Insert for Cutting Narrow Stock.

Resaw the band stock for #5 and #6 boxes on a band saw. Cut the wood slightly thicker than needed, then plane it or sand it to ³⁄₃₂" thick.

3/Slice the band stock for #0 to #4 boxes on a table saw. Feed the stock slowly, especially when cutting stock for the wider bands. Otherwise, the blade may heat and distort. This, in turn, will leave a ragged cut. **Saw guard removed for clarity.**

If you use a planer, you'll have to follow a special procedure. Ordinarily, most planers won't cut wood any thinner than ⅛"–1/16". To plane 3/32"-thick band stock, first plane a scrap, ½"–¾" thick and as long and as wide as the band stock. Cover one face of the scrap with spray adhesive, then sandwich the scrap and the stock together. Feed both pieces into the planer with the band stock on top. (See Figure 4.) When you've planed the band stock to the desired thickness, peel it off the scrap. Remove any spray adhesive with acetone.

Note: Make some extra band stock for each box. You may need it during the next steps.

4/To plane very thin stock, temporarily bond the wood on top of a scrap board. Surface the wood in several passes, taking very shallow cuts. This reduces the chance that the planer knives will peel the thin stock off the scrap and chew it up.

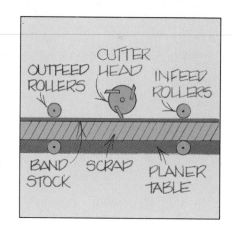

4 Cut and drill the swallowtail joints.

Cut the band stock to the lengths you need. Lay out swallowtail joints on one end of each band, as shown in the *Band Layouts*. Cut the joints with a band saw or a scroll saw. Drill 1/16"-diameter pilot holes through the swallowtails for driving tiny tacks.

TRY THIS! If you want to produce several boxes of the same size, stack the bands, one on top of the other, and tape them together. Lay out the joints on the top band, then saw and drill the swallowtails. Larry customarily produces the bands needed for 5 or 6 boxes in this manner.

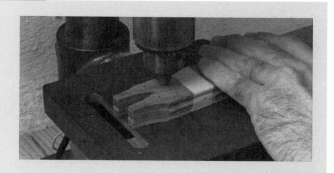

5 Bevel the edges of the swallowtails.

Using a very sharp utility knife or carving hook, cut bevels in the edges of the swallowtails. Start cutting at the base of each swallowtail, making the bevel very steep — about 60°. As you cut, make the bevel angle shallower and shallower. By the time you get to the end of the tail it should be 30°, as shown in the *Swallowtail Detail*. (See Figure 5.) Cut a bevel in the very end of each swallowtail, too.

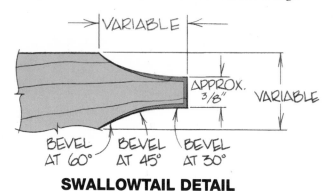

SWALLOWTAIL DETAIL

5/Cut the bevels in the edges of the swallowtail joints so they are steeper at the beginning of the tail than they are at the end. To do this, roll your wrist in one direction or the other as you cut.

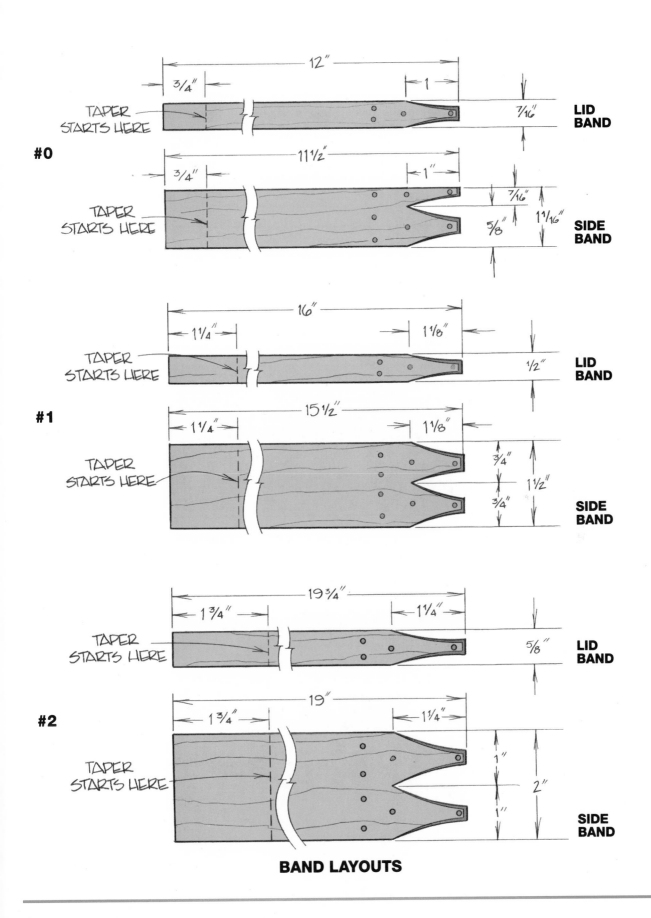

BAND LAYOUTS

6

Sand and taper the bands. On a stationary belt sander with a 100# sanding belt, sand the saw marks from each band. Grasp the band firmly so the sander doesn't pull it out of your hands. Keep the band moving as you work to sand the entire band evenly. Sand the swallowtails *slightly* thinner than the rest of the band. Then sand a taper on the opposite end of the band, as shown in the *Band Layouts*. (See Figure 6.)

6/Smooth each band on a belt sander, and sand a taper in the end opposite the swallowtails. Use a thin scrap to press the wood against the belt, as shown. This protects your fingers from the heat generated by the friction of sanding.

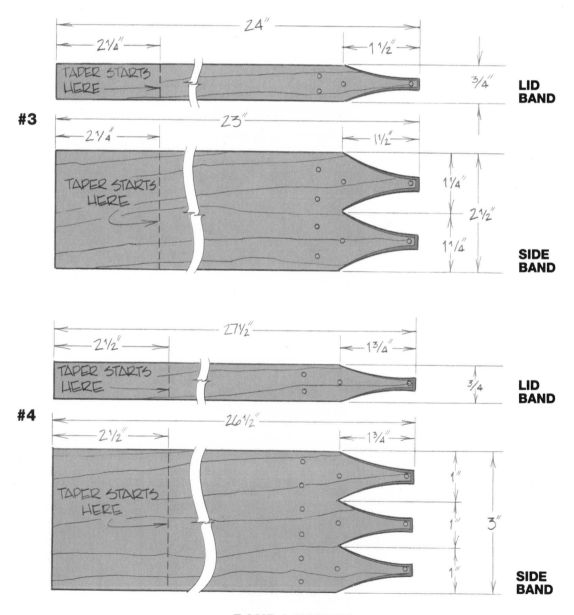

BAND LAYOUTS

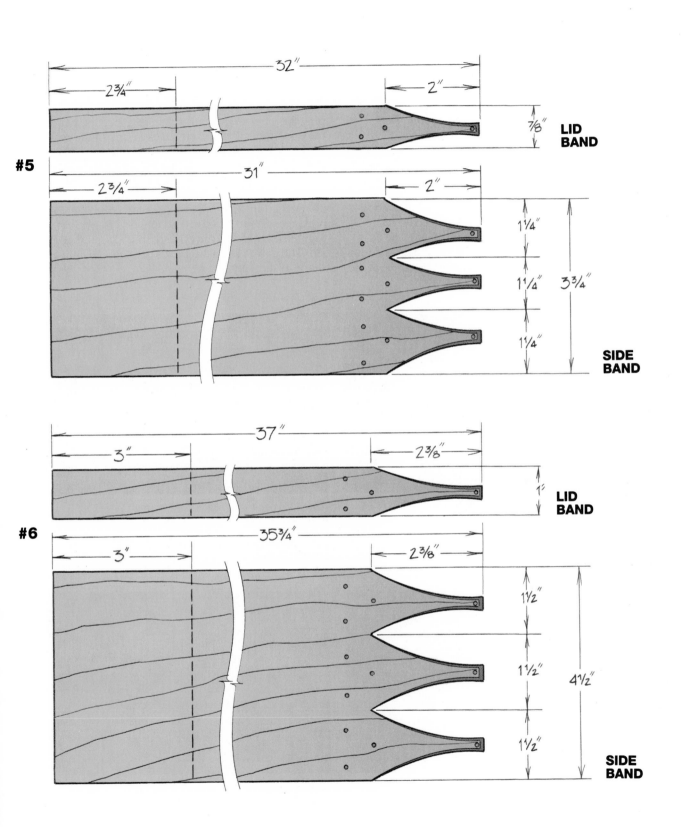

#5

2¾"

32"

2"

⅞"

LID
BAND

2¾"

31"

2"

1¼"

1¼"

3¾"

1¼"

SIDE
BAND

#6

3"

37"

2⅜"

1"

LID
BAND

3"

35¾"

2⅜"

1½"

1½"

4½"

1½"

SIDE
BAND

BAND LAYOUTS

7

Bend and fasten the side band. Fill the poacher with water. Turn on the hot plate and heat the water so it steams, but doesn't boil (about 150°F–175°F). Put the bands in the water and let them soak for at least 15 minutes, preferably 25. (You can soak them for longer without harming them, but they will take longer to dry.) When you take a band out of the water, it should be very pliable, no stiffer than shoe leather.

Take the side band out first. Before it cools, *quickly* bend it around the box mold. (See Figure 7.) Place the tapered end against the flat portion of the elliptical curve, and wrap it as tight as you can. Lap the swallowtails over the tapered end. *The swallowtails must end up on the flat portion of the curve, with the bevels facing up.* Mark the edges of the band across the lapped portion, near the base of the swallowtails. (See Figure 8.) Loosen the band just enough to take it off the mold, but don't let it come apart completely.

Note: If the wood breaks or splits when you bend it, you may not have soaked it long enough. It may also be too thick. Check it with calipers. However, sometimes the wood breaks no matter how long you soak it. This is one of the reasons you need to make extra band stock.

Lay the mold aside. Put the band back together, lapping the ends so the marks line up. Place the band over the end of the anvil. Insert a tack in one of the swallowtail holes and drive it home. (See Figure 9.) As the tack goes through the band, the point hits the metal anvil and clinches over. This keeps the tack from pulling loose. Repeat, driving tacks through all the holes.

Press the dryers into the assembled band like you'd press a cork into a bottle. Use two dryers, one at the top of the band and the other at the bottom. (See Figure 10.) The dryers keep the bands bent in an elliptical shape as they dry.

7/After soaking the bands for about 25 minutes, wrap the side band around the mold. You can use your bare hands; the wood shouldn't be that hot. If it is, wear leather gloves until the wood cools.

8/Mark the edge of the band across the lapped ends. This mark will help you put the band back together after you take it off the mold.

9/Drive the tacks so the points clinch over when they hit the metal anvil. Be careful not to drive them too hard. You don't want to pound the tack heads through the soft, wet wood. Larry prefers a small ball peen hammer for this operation: It helps him control just how hard he hits each tack.

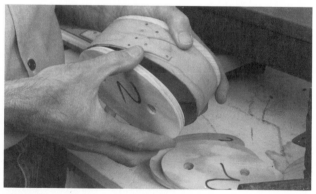

10/After you fasten the band in an elliptical loop, insert the dryers. Be careful not to force them in place; they should be snug, not tight. If you press too hard, the band may come apart.

8 **_Bend and fasten the lid band._** Take the lid band out of the poacher and wrap it around the assembled side band. Leave the dryers in place for this operation; they shouldn't be in the way. (See Figure 11.) Mark the lid band, remove it, and tack it together in the same manner as the side band. Then put it back in place around the side band. Adjust the top edge flush with the top of the side band, and turn it so all the swallowtails and tacks line up. Let both bands dry for several days.

11/To bend the lid band, use the assembled side band as a mold. After you fasten the lid band together, let it dry in place on the side band. This will ensure that the lid fits the box perfectly.

9 **_Cut and fit the bottom._** Make an oval-shaped bottom from ¼"-thick stock, cutting it to the shape shown in the *Lid/Bottom Patterns*. Cut ¹⁄₁₆"–⅛" wide of the line, then sand a 5° bevel in the edge, as shown in the *Lid/Bottom Edge Detail* — the same way you bevel-sanded the edges of the dryers. Don't sand up to the line yet; remain just wide of it.

Note: This bevel is very important. You should wedge the bottoms and the lids in the bands, not just insert them. The 5° bevel on the edge stretches the band slightly, making the joint tight all around the circumference.

Remove the dryers from the bands, and test fit the bottom in the side band. The fit should be snug, but you shouldn't have to force it. (Larry knows the parts fit properly when they squeak as he presses them together.) If the bottom is too tight, sand a little more stock from the edge and try again. Repeat until the bottom fits just right. (See Figure 12.) Press the bottom in place so the outside face is flush with the bottom edge of the band.

12/To fit the bottom to the side band, first place the flat part of the oval against the lapped ends of the band. Let the bottom swing into place, as if you were closing a door. This method puts a minimum of stress on the swallowtail joints.

LID/BOTTOM EDGE DETAIL

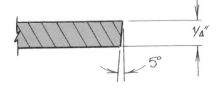

¼"

5°

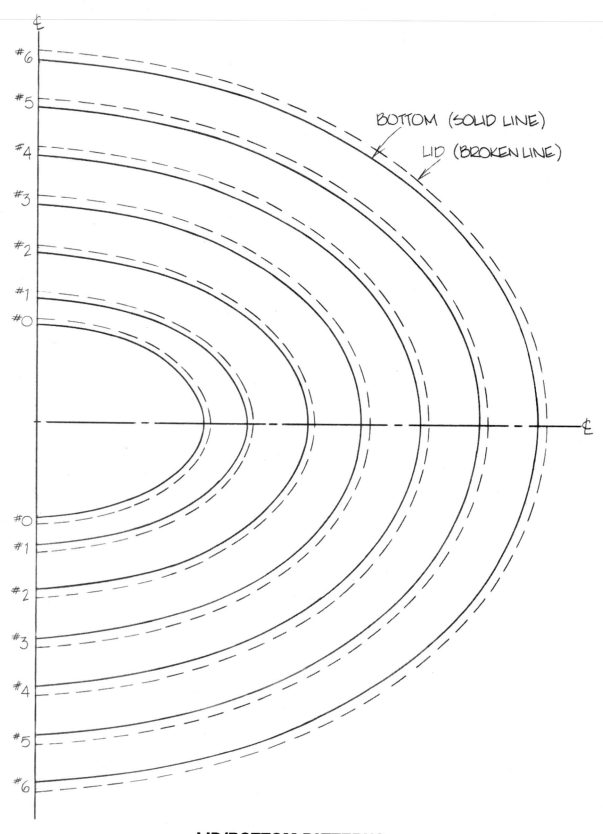

BOTTOM (SOLID LINE)

LID (BROKEN LINE)

LID/BOTTOM PATTERNS
(PRINTED AT 100%.)

10

Cut and fit the lid. Remove the lid band from the side band. Cut an oval-shaped lid and fit it to the band in the same manner as you fit the bottom. Place the lid assembly on the box and check that the swallowtail joints and the tacks line up. If the joints are misaligned, adjust the position of the band on the lid.

Mark the edge of the lid band just above the end of the lid swallowtail. Mark the lid just above the ends of the side swallowtails. (See Figure 13.) Remove the lid assembly from the box. Take the lid out of the band and put them back together, aligning the marks. Replace the lid on the box. The swallowtails should all line up. (See Figure 14.)

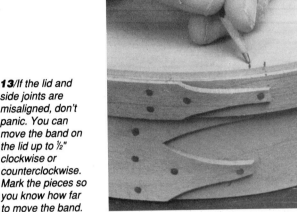

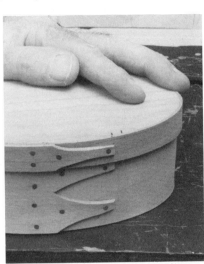

13/If the lid and side joints are misaligned, don't panic. You can move the band on the lid up to ½" clockwise or counterclockwise. Mark the pieces so you know how far to move the band.

14/Reassemble the lid and the band, then put the lid back on the box. The tacks and the edges of the swallowtails must line up. On some boxes, especially the larger ones, the lid may be loose on the box. The joints will only line up if you place the lid just so. If this is the case, use your best judgment when assembling the lid.

11

Peg the bottom and the lid to the bands. Drill ¹⁄₁₆"-diameter, ³⁄₈"-deep peg holes, ⅛" from the edge, all around the bottom of the box and the top of the lid. (See Figure 15.) These holes must go through the band and into the bottom or lid. Space them every 1"–2", but *don't* drill any holes at the points of the ellipse, where the curve is tightest. The wood is stressed at these points. If you drill a hole, you'll weaken the wood and it may break.

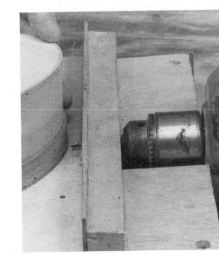

15/Drill ¹⁄₁₆"-diameter, ³⁄₈"-deep peg holes through the bands and into the lid or bottom. Larry made this drilling jig to help him position the holes and stop them at the proper depth.

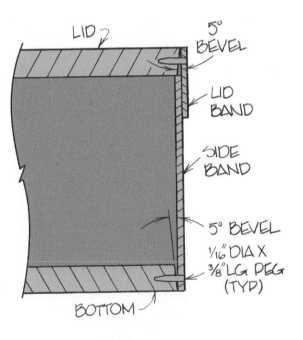

LID

5° BEVEL

LID BAND

SIDE BAND

5° BEVEL

¹⁄₁₆" DIA X ³⁄₈" LG PEG (TYP)

BOTTOM

JOINERY DETAIL

Use ordinary round toothpicks for the pegs. Clip them in half with a pair of wire cutters to make two pegs from each. Dip the smaller end of a peg in glue and insert it in a peg hole. If it seems loose, trim a little off the point and try the fit again. Continue until you have filled all the holes. (See Figure 16.) Let the glue dry, then use a utility knife to trim the pegs flush with the wood surface.

16/Use round toothpicks as pegs to fasten the bottom and lid in place. You may have to trim ¼"–⅜" off the pointed ends so they won't be loose in the peg holes.

12 Sand and finish the boxes.

Sand and finish the boxes. Sand all the surfaces clean and flush. (Larry uses a belt sander to do this, pressing very lightly so he doesn't sand through the thin bands.) If you wish to paint the boxes, don't bother finish sanding them. Apply a milk paint or latex paint to the rough-sanded surface.

If you want to apply a clear finish, sand the surfaces on the *outside* of the box with fine (120#) or very fine (180#) sandpaper. When the wood is as smooth as you think it ought to be, apply a finish to the outside of the box only. The inside of the box should be left unfinished, so the wood will absorb moisture and keep the contents from mildewing.

Variations

*O*val boxes also were used without lids as caddies or carriers.

To make a divided carrier, cut a divider from ¼"-thick stock, as shown in the *Divider Layout*. The divider should be no higher than the side band, and stretch lengthwise across the bottom. Cut a slot near the top for a hand grip. Glue the divider to the bottom, and peg it to the side band.

To make a carrier with a *handle,* cut a 1"-wide handle from band stock. Experiment with a paper template to figure how long to make the handle.

Generally, you want the handle to extend the same distance above the bottom as the box is long. Cut the handle to length and poach it. When it's limber, fasten it to the side band with tacks in the same manner that you assembled the bands. The handle should run side to side, between the flat portions of the elliptical curve. Let it dry for several days before you sand and finish the basket.

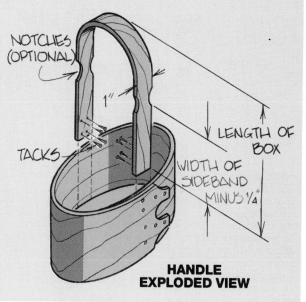

DIVIDER LAYOUT

HANDLE EXPLODED VIEW

Step-by-Step: Drawing an Oval

*O*ccasionally, the Shakers made nests of as many as twelve oval boxes. Some were smaller and some larger than those shown in the "Shaker Oval Boxes" chapter. Should you want to add boxes to your nest — or make oval boxes of sizes other than the patterns given — you must first draw an oval pattern for the molds, dryers, bottoms, and lids. Here is a method for drawing an oval (or an ellipse) to the precise size you need:

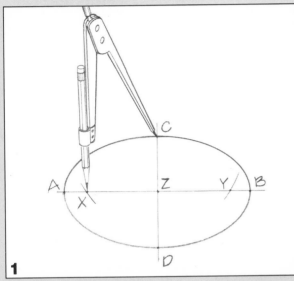

1

Mark the length or **major axis** (AB) and the width or **minor axis** (CD) of the oval on a sheet of paper. The axes must be perpendicular to each other and cross at the center (Z). Adjust a compass to half the length of the major axis (AZ or ZB). Put the point of the compass on one end of the minor axis (C or D), and scribe arcs that intersect the major axis (at X and Y).

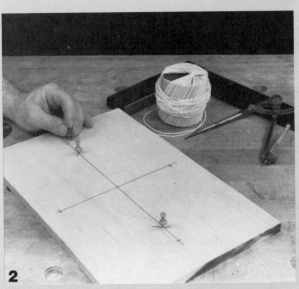

2

Drive two tacks or small nails at the points where the arcs intersect the major axis (X and Y). Put a third tack at one end of the major axis (A or B), so all three tacks are in a line.

3

Loop a length of string around the line of tacks, and tie the ends together in a square knot.

4

Remove the tack at the end of the major axis (A or B) but leave the string and the other tacks in place. Put the point of a pencil through the square knot and stretch the string taut. Draw the oval, keeping the string taut and pulling it around the tacks.

Butter Press

Like so many traditional country artifacts, the butter press is a marriage of beauty and utility. This old-time kitchen utensil was made to portion butter into small, equal pats. It operates in a simple, no-nonsense fashion — press cold butter into the barrel, push the plunger, and out comes a single pat. But the head of the plunger has a tiny, incised carving. This imparts a raised decoration to each pat, and adds a little ornament to an otherwise strictly functional device.

The presses shown were designed and made by Dick Belcher, a professional carver and carving instructor from Dayton, Ohio. He shaped the parts — barrel, shaft, and plunger — on a lathe, then carved a four-leaf clover design into the plunger. There are many traditional country designs for butter presses, but Dick prefers the clover for its simplicity. Not only is it easy to carve, it reproduces well in the butter. Complex shapes, he finds, lose clarity. ●

**EXPLODED
VIEW**

Materials List

FINISHED DIMENSIONS

PARTS

A. Barrel   1⅝" dia. x 1⅝"
B. Shaft   ¾" dia. x 2¼"
C. Plunger   1⅛" dia. x ⅝"

---

1 *Select and prepare the stock.* Traditionally, butter presses are made from a hard, close-grained wood. Rock maple is the most common choice, but you can also use cherry, birch, and apple. Avoid other species, particularly those with an open grain, for a couple of reasons. When you use a butter press, you must soak it in hot water periodically. Open-grained wood will absorb water quickly. This, in turn, may cause the piece to swell and crack. An open grain also

absorbs the oils from the butter, making the press hard to clean.

Cut the stock into turning squares. For a single butter press, you'll need squares measuring 1" x 1" x 4" to make the shaft, 1¼" x 1¼" x 2½" to make the plunger, and 1⅞" x 1⅞" x 2½" to make the barrel. Remember that the grain of a turning square should be parallel to the axis of rotation. Squares with the grain perpendicular to rotation are difficult to turn.

---

2 *Drill holes in the barrel.* Hollow out the barrel and drill the shaft hole *before* you mount the stock on the lathe. Use a 1¼"-diameter multi-spur bit or Forstner bit to drill the 1"-deep hollow — both of these bits drill holes with smooth, clean sides and flat bottoms. Work slowly, with the drill press turning at a slow speed. If you run the bit too fast when drilling end grain, it will burn the wood. The larger the bit, the slower you must run the tool to prevent this.

Switch to an ordinary ⁷⁄₁₆"-diameter bit to make the shaft hole. Locate the center of the hollow. This shouldn't be hard to find — most multi-spur and Forstner bits have a pilot in the center that leaves a small indentation. When you find the center, drill the shaft hole ¾" deep. *Don't* drill completely through the stock. The shaft hole will open up when you trim the waste from the turned barrel.

3 **Turn the parts.** Mount the parts on a lathe, and spindle-turn each part to the dimensions shown in the *Plunger Details, Shaft Detail,* and *Barrel Details.* To mount the hollowed-out barrel stock, cut a 1¼"-diameter, 2"-long plug that fits the hollow. Place the stock between the centers with the plug in place. (See Figure 1.) The pressure of the lathe centers will hold the plug in place while you turn the shape of the barrel.

After shaping, finish sand each part on the lathe. Remove the plug from the barrel and cut away the waste from the top end. Also cut away the waste from both ends of the shaft. Leave the waste attached to the plunger for the moment.

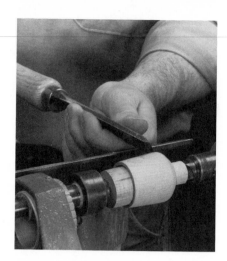

1/Put a plug in the hollow so you can mount the barrel stock between lathe centers. Cut this plug from scrap or make it from a short length of 1¼"-diameter closet pole.

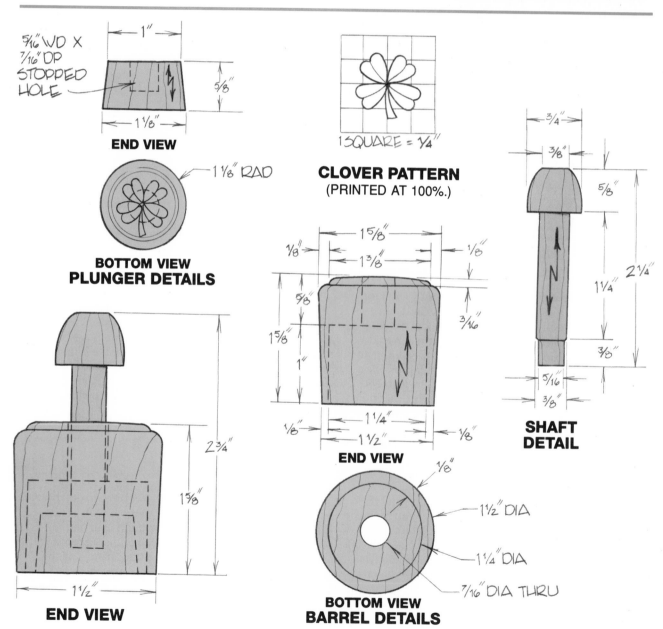

5⁄16" WD X 7⁄16" DP STOPPED HOLE

1"

5⁄8"

1⅛"

END VIEW

1⅛" RAD

BOTTOM VIEW
PLUNGER DETAILS

2¾"

1⅝"

1½"

END VIEW

CLOVER PATTERN
(PRINTED AT 100%.)

1 SQUARE = ¼"

1⁄8"

1⅝"

1⅜"

1⁄8"

5⁄8"

1⅝"

3⁄16"

1"

1⁄8"

1¼"

1½"

1⁄8"

END VIEW

1⁄8"

1½" DIA

1¼" DIA

7⁄16" DIA THRU

BOTTOM VIEW
BARREL DETAILS

¾"

⅜"

5⁄8"

2¼"

1¼"

⅜"

5⁄16"

⅜"

SHAFT DETAIL

4 Drill the mortise and carve the design in the plunger.

Drill the mortise and carve the design in the plunger. Mount the plunger back on the lathe. With the point of a skew chisel, make a narrow groove in the bottom, about ⅛" in from the circumference. (See Figure 2.) Dismount the plunger and trim the waste from both ends. Drill a ⁵⁄₁₆"-diameter round mortise, ⁷⁄₁₆" deep, in the top so you can attach the plunger to the shaft.

Sketch a four-leaf clover on the bottom of the plunger, loosely following the *Clover Pattern*. Using a small gouge, hollow out the leaves. (See Figure 3.) Finally, make the stem with a small V-shaped chisel. Make sure all your carving tools are razor sharp, and touch up the cutting edges often as you work. Because you're carving end grain, the incised surface of the clover will be very ragged if you use dull tools. This, in turn, will cause the butter to stick to the plunger. You won't be able to mold a good, crisp clover shape. Sharp tools cut the end grain cleanly; the incised surface is smooth; and the butter molds easily.

2/Using a skew chisel, score a V-shaped groove in the bottom of the plunger, near the circumference. Cut the groove about ¹⁄₁₆" deep and ¹⁄₁₆" wide, no more.

3/Carve the leaves about ⅛" deep and the stem about ¹⁄₁₆" deep. Don't carve them any deeper, or the butter may stick in the mold.

5 Assemble the butter press.

Assemble the butter press. Do any necessary touch-up sanding on the parts, then dry assemble them. Check that they fit together properly and that the shaft and plunger will slide smoothly in and out of the barrel. When you're satisfied they do, disassemble the project.

Dip the parts in a nontoxic "salad bowl" finish made especially for wooden kitchen utensils. This finish soaks into the wood and keeps it from absorbing water, oil, or most other liquids. Various brands are available through craft stores and mail-order woodworking suppliers.

When the finish dries, lightly buff the parts with 0000# steel wool. Insert the shaft through the hole in the barrel. Glue the end of the shaft in the top of the plunger. Use a waterproof glue, such as epoxy or resorcinol.

Using the Butter Press

Molding butter in a butter press is an art — perhaps a more difficult art than making the press itself. If you intend to use your press, here are some guidelines:

■ Work with *very cold* butter. Put it in the freezer for several hours before making the pats.

■ Fill a bowl with hot tap water. Put the press in the water to soak for a few minutes before making each pat.

■ Cut or scoop a small amount of butter off the block — just a little more than you need to make a pat. Knead it for just a *few seconds* to make it malleable.

■ Quickly press the butter in the barrel, then quickly press the plunger to remove the pat.

The warm press melts the surface of the cold butter and allows the pat to separate easily, leaving a distinct clover shape. If you let the butter stay in the press too long, the pat will melt and the clover will be indistinct. If the press is too cold or the butter too warm, the butter will stick to the plunger. It takes some practice to get good clover shapes consistently. Your materials have to be at the proper temperature, and your timing has to be just right.

Door Harp

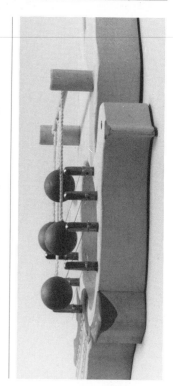

Like most country devices, the door harp was a practical invention. It let you know, gently and unobtrusively, when someone was entering or leaving a room. Shopkeepers hung them on store entrances so they would know when customers came calling. Parents used them to monitor the whereabouts of small children. Cooks sometimes used harps to booby-trap pantry doors, warning them of raids on their baked goods. But the door harp was fanciful, too. Its sweet, soft music transformed the everyday act of opening a door into a quiet celebration.

A door harp makes music in the same manner as a piano. The strings are stretched across a sounding board and tuned to different notes. A wooden bead hangs beside each string suspended by a thread. The instrument is secured to a door. When the door is opened or closed, the movement of the door causes the beads to hammer the strings, creating a pleasant, tinkling sound — much like a cat walking across the upper registers of a piano.

Door harps came in many shapes and sizes; the one shown was made in the shape of a dove — the traditional symbol for harmony. However, you can make yours to any pattern you prefer. Simply cut a hole in the center of the sounding board, then mount the strings and the beads as shown in the drawings.

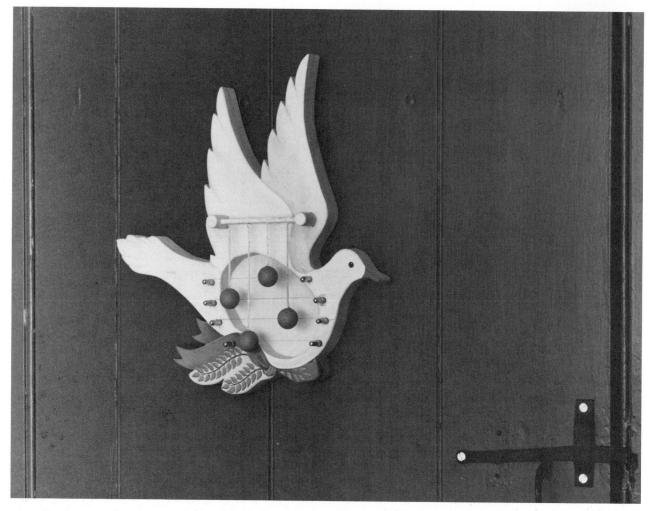

Materials List

FINISHED DIMENSIONS

PARTS

A.	Sounding board	3/4" x 11⅛" x 10⅞"
B.	Back	⅛" x 10⅛" x 11⅞"
C.	Posts (2)	½" dia. x 1½"
D.	Rail	¼" dia. x 3¾"
E.	Beads (4)	¾" dia.

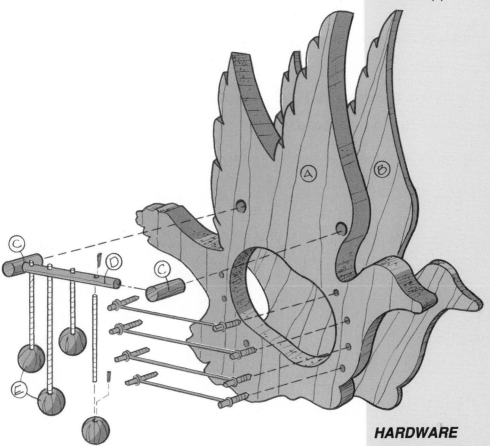

EXPLODED VIEW

HARDWARE

Autoharp pegs* (8)
.011 Banjo string*
.012 Banjo string*
Nylon string (16")
Round toothpicks (4–8)

*These pegs and banjo strings can be purchased at most musical instrument stores. If the salesperson asks, it doesn't matter whether you buy "ball-end" or "loop-end" strings; you're going to cut the ends off anyway. The pegs may have to be specially ordered through the store.

1 Select the stock and cut it to size.
Choose a hard or medium-hard wood for the sounding board and back. The wood must grip the autoharp pegs tightly and prevent them from turning. Maple, birch, and poplar will all work well, but avoid pine, cedar, and other softwoods. In a soft wood, the tension on the strings pulls the pegs sideways. The holes become enlarged, the pegs come loose, and the strings go slack. They won't hold the note that you tune them to.

After selecting the stock, plane it to the thicknesses you need — ¾" for the sounding board and ⅛" for the back. Cut these parts to size. Make the posts and rail from commercial dowel stock, and purchase the beads from an arts-and-crafts store or a mail-order woodworking supplier.

2 Cut the shapes of the sounding board and back.
Stack the sounding board on the back and tape the two pieces together. Enlarge the pattern and trace it on the sounding board. Cut the shape with a band saw or scroll saw, and remove the tape.

Set the back aside for the moment. Drill a ¼"-diameter hole through the sounding board, within the outline of the sound hole. Insert the blade of a saber saw or scroll saw in the small hole, then cut out the sound hole. Sand the inside edge of the sound hole, but don't bother to sand the outside edge of the sounding board or back just yet. You'll sand these edges *after* you assemble the parts.

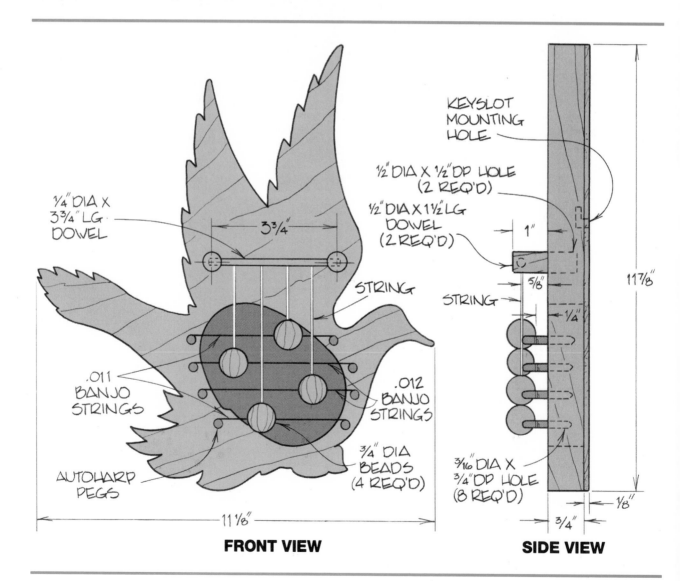

FRONT VIEW **SIDE VIEW**

3

Drill the holes. To assemble the harp, you must drill several different-sized holes in the various parts. Here's a list:

- ½"-diameter, ½"-deep holes in the sounding board to hold the posts, as shown in the *Side View* and *Front View*
- ¼"-diameter, ⅜"-deep holes near the top ends of the posts, as shown in the *Post Layout,* to hold the rail
- ³⁄₁₆"-diameter, ¾"-deep holes arranged around the sound hole, as shown in the *Front View,* to hold the autoharp pegs
- ⅛"-diameter holes through the rail, as shown in the *Rail Layout,* to suspend the beads

- ⅛"-diameter, ⅜"-deep holes in the beads to hold the end of the string

TRY THIS! The easiest way to get a small bead to lie still when you're drilling it is to make a cradle for it. Bore a hole slightly smaller than the diameter of the bead in a piece of scrap wood. Place the bead in the hole to drill it. The pressure of the bit will keep the bead in the hole while you work.

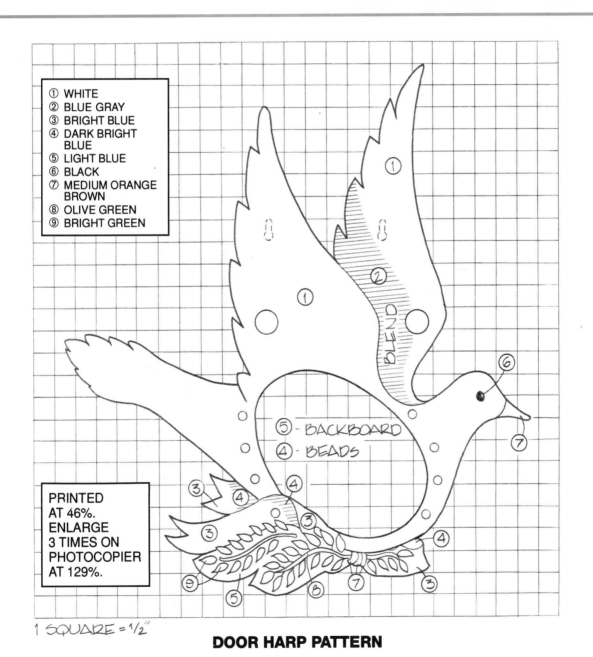

① WHITE
② BLUE GRAY
③ BRIGHT BLUE
④ DARK BRIGHT BLUE
⑤ LIGHT BLUE
⑥ BLACK
⑦ MEDIUM ORANGE BROWN
⑧ OLIVE GREEN
⑨ BRIGHT GREEN

BLEND

⑤ - BACKBOARD
④ - BEADS

PRINTED AT 46%. ENLARGE 3 TIMES ON PHOTOCOPIER AT 129%.

1 SQUARE = ½"

DOOR HARP PATTERN

4 **Assemble the harp.** Finish sand the sounding board, back, posts, and rail. Glue the back to the sounding board, then sand the edges clean and flush. Rout two key-slot mounting holes in the back, one in each wing. The slots should be aligned vertically with the holes at their bases, as shown in the *Door Harp Pattern*. (See Figures 1 and 2.) These specially shaped mounting holes secure the harp to the door, yet let you remove it easily.

Glue the rail in the posts, then glue the posts in the sounding board. Take care that the ⅛"-diameter holes in the rail are *parallel* to the face of the sounding board.

1/To make a key-slot mounting hole, you need a special key-slot cutter for a router. Mount the bit so it protrudes about ³⁄₈" below the base of the router. Turn the router on and lower it onto the stock, boring a hole with the cutter.

2/After boring the hole, cut the slot. Slowly slide the router ½"–1" in a straight line. Turn the router off, let it come to a complete stop, and remove the cutter from the mounting hole.

5 **Insert the strings in the beads.** Cut four nylon strings about 4" long. This is much longer than you need, but it will give you plenty of extra string for assembly and adjustment. Burn the ends of each string with a match to prevent them from unraveling.

Insert one end of a string in the ⅛"-diameter hole in a bead. Dip the point of a round toothpick in glue, then press it in the hole to securely wedge the string. (See Figure 3.) Break the toothpick off flush with the surface of the bead, and repeat for the other beads.

3/Wedge a string in each bead with a toothpick, as shown. If the point of the toothpick is too slender to wedge itself in the hole, trim ¼"–³⁄₈" off the narrower end. It must fit tightly enough to keep the string from pulling loose.

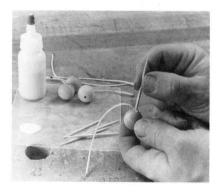

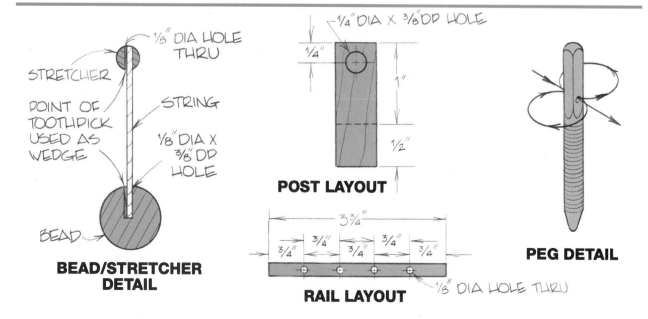

⅛" DIA HOLE THRU

STRETCHER

POINT OF TOOTHPICK USED AS WEDGE

STRING

⅛" DIA X ³⁄₈" DP HOLE

BEAD

BEAD/STRETCHER DETAIL

¼" DIA X ³⁄₈" DP HOLE

¼"

1"

½"

POST LAYOUT

3 ¾"

¾"   ¾"   ¾"   ¾"   ¾"

RAIL LAYOUT

⅛" DIA HOLE THRU

PEG DETAIL

6 **Finish the door harp and beads.** Do any necessary touch-up sanding, then paint or apply a finish to the wooden surfaces. If you choose to paint this project, use latex or acrylic colors. To give the colors an antique look, apply a thin coat of *tinted* shellac over the paint. Tint the shellac with burnt umber artist's oil paint; this will artificially age the color of the finish. (Artist's oils can be purchased at most paint stores and arts-and-crafts stores.)

7 **Install and tune the banjo strings.** Drive the autoharp pegs into the ³⁄₁₆"-diameter holes in the sounding board, turning them as if they were small lag screws. Stop turning when the hole in each peg is approximately ¼" above the surface of the board.

Cut the ball or loop end off each banjo string and then cut it in two. Install the .011 strings between the two sets of pegs that are *closest together* (those at top and bottom), and the .012 strings between the two sets that are *furthest apart* (those in the middle). Insert each end of each string through a peg. Loop the end clock wise around the peg and back through the hole. Then take it counterclockwise around the peg and back through the hole for a third time, as shown in the *Peg Detail*. This will prevent the string from coming loose on the peg.

Turn the pegs slowly, tightening the strings. Tune the strings to a chord — base note, third, fifth, and octave. Use the .012 strings for the two lowest notes in the chord, and the .011 strings for the two highest notes. If you don't have the musical expertise to do this, find someone who does to help you.

8 **Hang the beads from the rail.** Clamp the door harp in a vise so the sounding board is vertical and the banjo strings are horizontal — as if the harp were hanging on a door. Insert the ends of the nylon strings (that the beads are attached to) through the ⅛" holes in the rail. Pull each string through its hole, adjusting the height of the bead. Suspend a bead beside each banjo string, as shown in the *Front View*.

Wedge the strings in the rail with toothpicks, in the same manner that you wedged them in the beads. (See Figure 4.) Break the toothpicks off flush with the surface of the rail, and cut off the excess string.

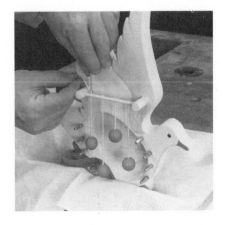

4/When you have adjusted a bead to the desired height, wedge the string in the rail with the point of a toothpick. If the point protrudes from the rail, trim a little off the point. Dip the toothpick in glue, so the wedge stays put.

9 **Hang the door harp.** Use two flathead wood screws, about 1" long, to mount the harp to the door. Most key-slot mounting holes require #10 or #12 screws. However, depending on the brand of cutter used, you may need another size. The head of the screw should be wider than the slot, but able to fit into the hole at the base of the slot.

Measure and mark the positions of the screws on the door. They should be level, and as far apart as the key-slot mounting holes. Drill pilot holes, then drive the screws into the door so the heads protrude ¼" to ⅜".

Place the door harp over the screws, fitting the heads into the bases of the key-slot mounting holes. Slide the harp down so the screws enter the slots. If the screws seem tight, remove the harp and back the screw out slightly. If they are too loose, drive them in further. Be careful not to chip or break the edges of the slots.

Miniature Chest of Drawers

An eighteenth- or nineteenth-century cabinetmaker sometimes made a miniature model, about one-third scale, before he began work on a large furniture piece. This helped the cabinetmaker refine the design, and the model showed a client what he was buying. When the full-scale piece was finished, the cabinetmaker usually presented the miniature along with it. This delighted the client, who got two pieces of furniture for the price of one.

Because of this practice, miniature furniture became a common sight in many better-appointed homes. Some pieces were displayed as curios, but most saw as much use as full-sized furniture. A miniature often made an excellent storage unit for small items — jewelry, writing materials, silverware, and so on. The small chest of drawers shown was made in the early nineteenth century as a model for a large four-drawer storage chest. Later, the owner adapted it to hold sewing notions. The drawers have dividers to help organize spools, bobbins, needles, and pins.

Although this miniature is made to the same proportions as a full-sized piece,

it is much easier to build. The purpose of a miniature was to test the design, not the joinery. The construction is greatly simplified. The craftsman who made this small chest eliminated the web frames and other traditional bracework that he probably used on the larger piece. The drawers slide on simple guides, tacked to the sides. The base assembly is mitered and screwed in place — there are no splines or glue blocks to reinforce it. Only the drawers are built with the same joinery as full-sized furniture.

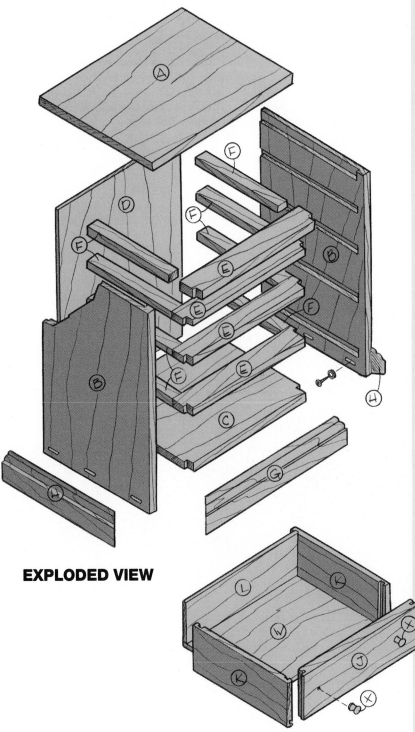

EXPLODED VIEW

Materials List

FINISHED DIMENSIONS

PARTS

A. Top   ½" x 8½" x 12"

B. Sides (2)   ½" x 8" x 12"

C. Bottom   ⅜" x 7¾" x 10½"

D. Back   ¼" x 10½" x 12"

E. Rails (4)   ⅜" x 1¼" x 10½"

F. Drawer guides (8)   ⅜" x ¾" x 6½"

G. Front molding   ½" x 1⅞" x 12"

H. Side moldings (2)   ½" x 1⅞" x 8½"

J. Bottom drawer front   ½" x 2¹³⁄₁₆" x 9⅞"

K. Bottom drawer sides (2)   ¼" x 2¹³⁄₁₆" x 7⅝"

L. Bottom drawer back   ¼" x 2⁷⁄₁₆" x 9⅝"

M. Lower middle drawer front   ½" x 2⁵⁄₁₆" x 9⅞"

N. Lower middle drawer sides (2)   ¼" x 2⁵⁄₁₆" x 7⅝"

P. Lower middle drawer back   ¼" x 1¹⁵⁄₁₆" x 9⅝"

Q. Upper middle drawer front   ½" x 1³⁄₁₆" x 9⅞"

R. Upper middle drawer sides (2)   ¼" x 1¹³⁄₁₆" x 7⅝"

S. Upper middle drawer back   ¼" x 1⁷⁄₁₆" x 9⅝"

T. Top drawer front   ½" x 1⁵⁄₁₆" x 9⅞"

U. Top drawer sides (2)   ¼" x 1⁵⁄₁₆" x 7⅝"

V. Top drawer back   ¼" x ¹⁵⁄₁₆" x 9⅝"

W. Drawer bottoms (4)   ¼" x 7⅛" x 9⅝"

X. Drawer pulls (8)   ½" dia. x ¹³⁄₁₆"

HARDWARE

¾" Wire brads (48–60)

1" Wire brads (16–20)

#8 x ¾" Roundhead wood screws and flat washers (6)

1 **Select the wood and cut the parts.** This project is small enough to be made from scrap wood. The antique chest probably *was* made from scraps; cabinetmakers didn't often waste good wood on models. You can use a variety of woods that you may have lying about your shop — walnut, cherry, maple, and pine were the most common materials of the country cabinetmaker. The chest shown is built of sugar maple and white pine.

Once you have selected the wood, plane it to the thicknesses needed — ½" for the sides, top, molding, and drawer fronts, ⅜" for the drawer guides, rails, and bottom, and ¼" for the back, drawer sides, drawer backs, and drawer bottoms. Cut all the parts to size

except the moldings and drawer pulls. Rip the moldings to the proper width, but don't cut them to length yet. Don't do anything with the drawer pull stock for the moment.

> TRY THIS!   Many cabinetmakers prefer to build drawers ¹⁄₁₆"-⅛" oversize, then plane and sand them to fit. This takes a little patience, especially when you make several drawers, but you can get a much better fit.

2 **Cut the joinery in the sides.** Rout the rabbets and dadoes in the side stock, as shown in the *Left Side Layout*. Use a straightedge or a T-shaped jig to guide the router. The horizontal (side-to-side) rabbets and dadoes should be *blind:* Stop the router ½" short of the front edge so the cuts won't show from the front of the chest. Square the blind ends with a chisel.

Note: Remember that the sides must be mirror images of each other. The joinery on the right side should be the reverse of the left.

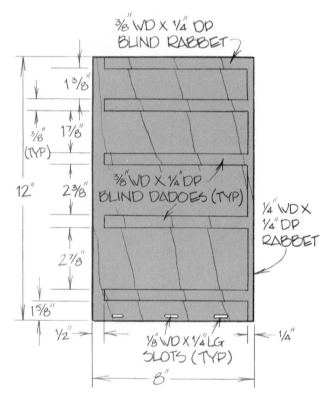

**LEFT SIDE
LAYOUT**

3 **Drill the slots in the sides.** The wood grain of the side moldings runs perpendicular to that of the sides. Because of this, you must fasten the two parts so the sides can expand and contract freely. Otherwise, the joints will pop or the chest will distort. To let the wood move, use sliding screw joints — the

screws slide back and forth in ¼"-long slots as the wood shrinks and swells. Make each slot by drilling several overlapping ⅛"-diameter holes. Place three slots in each side near the bottom edge, as shown in the *Left Side Layout.*

4

Cut the joinery in the bottom and the rails. Using a band saw or dovetail saw, cut ¼"-wide, ½"-long notches in the front corners of the bottom and the rails, as shown in the *Bottom Layout* and

Drawer Guide Layout. Test fit these parts in the blind dadoes and rabbets you cut in the sides. When assembled, the front edges of all parts — sides, rails, and bottom — should be flush.

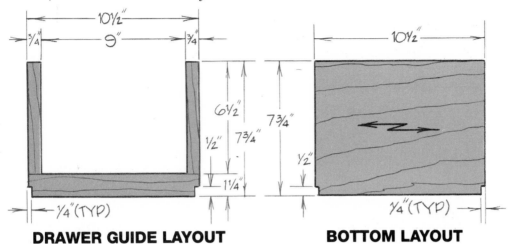

DRAWER GUIDE LAYOUT

BOTTOM LAYOUT

TOP VIEW

SECTION A

FRONT VIEW

SIDE VIEW

5 **Assemble the case.** Lightly sand all parts of the case (except the moldings), and finish sand the sides and top. Tack (but *don't* glue) the drawer guides in place in the blind rabbets and dadoes, using ¾" wire brads. Drive these brads at a steep angle, through the top face of the guides and into the sides, as shown in the *Case Joinery Detail*. This way, you won't see them on the outside of the chest.

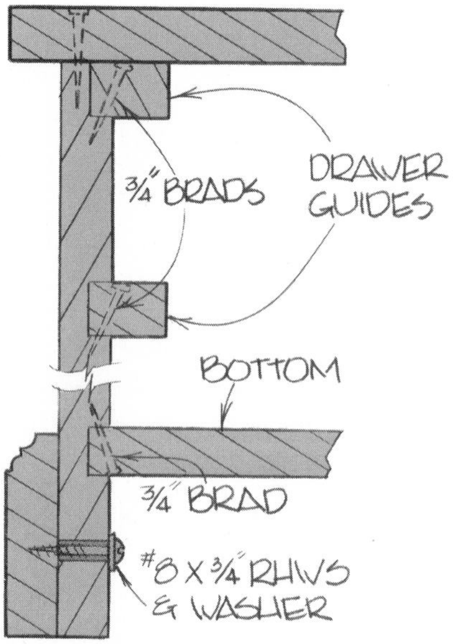

Note: The grain of the guides is perpendicular to that of the sides. If you glue the guides in place, they will create the same problems mentioned earlier — the joints pop and the case distorts as the sides expand and contract. The brads bend slightly as the sides move, preventing this from happening.

Glue the sides, rails, and bottom together. Reinforce the bottom-to-side joint with ¾" brads, driving them through the bottom and into the sides, as was done to hold the guides.

Tack (but don't glue) the back and the top to the assembly. Use ¾" brads to attach the back, and 1" brads for the top. As you work, vary the angle at which you drive the brads. This will help anchor the parts in place. (See Figure 1.) After you drive the brads, set the heads slightly below the surface of the wood.

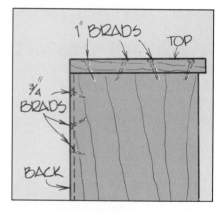

*1/When attaching the top and the back, alternate the angle of the brads front-to-back or top-to-bottom to help secure the parts. Do **not** vary the angle from side to side, or the points of the brads may come through the sides.*

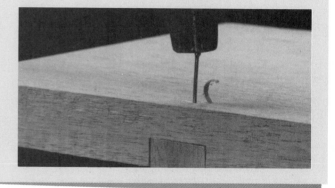

CASE JOINERY DETAIL

(labels: ¾" BRADS, DRAWER GUIDES, BOTTOM, ¾" BRAD, #8 X ¾" RHWS & WASHER)

TRY THIS! To hide the heads of the brads that hold the top to the case, use a *blind nail plane*. Select a spot where you want to drive a brad, and lift a curl of wood with the plane. Drive the brad into the hollow left by the curl and set the head. Glue the curl back in place, let the glue dry, and lightly sand the area. You won't be able to tell there's a nail under the surface of the wood!

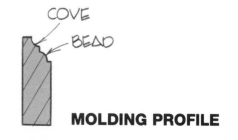

6 **Make and attach the molding.** Shape the top edge of the molding stock, using a table-mounted router. The shape shown in the *Molding Profile* is a traditional bead-and-cove, or "bed molding." (In tool catalogs, this is often referred to as a "classic molding" shape.) You can make this shape or any other that suits your fancy.

(labels: COVE, BEAD)

MOLDING PROFILE

Cut the moldings to length, mitering the adjoining ends. Glue the front molding to the assembly first, then attach the side pieces. Glue the mitered ends of the side moldings to the front, but *do not apply glue to any other portion of the side moldings.* To hold these parts to the case, drive roundhead wood screws with flat washers through the side slots and into the moldings. Tighten the screws, but don't turn them so tight that they press the washers into the wood.

Reinforce the miter joints with 1" brads, as shown in Figure 2. Drive the brads at right angles to each other, from both the front and the side. This not only keeps the miter joints from pulling apart, but also helps to hold the front molding in place.

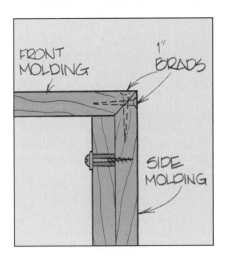

2/Reinforce the miter joints with brads, driving them at right angles to each other. If you wish, use a blind nail plane to hide the heads of the brads.

7

Cut the drawer joinery. Lock joints hold the drawer fronts to the sides; dadoes hold the backs; and the bottoms rest in grooves, as shown in the *Bottom Drawer Details.* You can make all of these joints on a table saw or a table-mounted router.

To make a lock joint, first cut a ⅛"-wide, ⅛"-deep dado in the inside face of the drawer side, ⅛" from the front end. (See Figure 3.) Next, cut a ¼"-wide, ¼"-deep groove in the adjoining end of the drawer front. (See Figure 4.) This will create two fingers or tenons on the end of the workpiece. Trim the *inside* tenon — the tenon on the back face of the drawer front — to a length of ⅛". (See Figure 5.) This short tenon must fit snugly in the dado you cut in the drawer side.

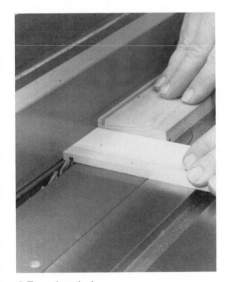

3/To make a lock joint, first cut a dado on the inside face of the drawer side. If you're using a table saw, make the cut with a combination blade — the kerf will be exactly ⅛" wide.

4/Cut a groove in the end of the drawer front, still using the combination blade, in two passes. Feed the ½"-thick workpiece over the blade, making a ⅛"-wide kerf, ⅛" from the face of the board. Turn the board edge-for-edge and make another pass, widening the kerf to ¼". You can make a jig to keep the stock from slipping down between the blade and the table; see the section on *Making a Table Saw Insert for Cutting Narrow Stock* for instructions.

*5/The ¼"-wide kerf, centered in the end of the drawer front, will create two ⅛"- wide tenons — one on either side of the kerf. Trim the **inside** tenon so it fits the dado in the drawer side. Clamp a stop block on the rip fence to position the drawer front on the saw. This block* also keeps the work from binding between the blade and the fence.

8 **Make the drawer pulls.** Turn eight drawer pulls, following the *Drawer Pull Pattern*. If you don't have a lathe, you can use a drill press to make the turnings. To do this, you must build the attachment shown in the Drill Press Turning Jig section. Clamp it to the drill press table directly beneath the chuck. Cut a length of ½"-diameter dowel for turning stock, and mount it *vertically*. Clamp the upper end in the chuck and rest the lower end on the pivot, as shown in Figure 6. Turn the pulls at a low speed.

To mount the pulls, drill ¼"-diameter holes in the drawer fronts, 2" in from each end and centered top-to-bottom, as shown in the *Bottom Drawer Details/ Front View*. These mounting holes must line up vertically when the drawers are in place, as shown in the *Front View*.

6/If you don't have a lathe, use a drill press and a lathe jig to turn the drawer pulls. You can turn up to four pulls at once, using a piece of ½"-diameter dowel stock, 7"–8" long. As you work, oil the metal pivot occasionally to keep the stock turning smoothly.

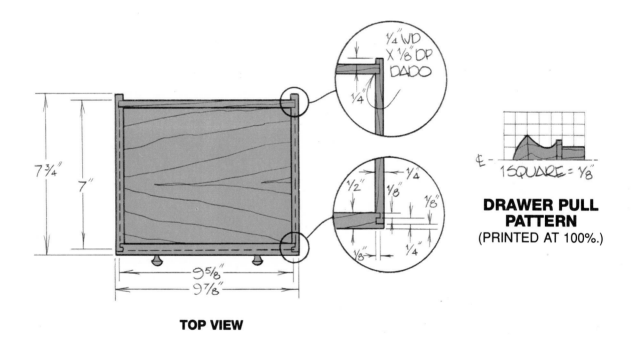

TOP VIEW

DRAWER PULL PATTERN
(PRINTED AT 100%.)

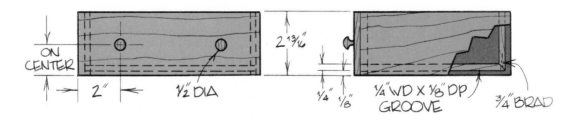

FRONT VIEW   **SIDE VIEW**

BOTTOM DRAWER DETAILS

9 **Assemble and fit the drawers.** Finish sand all the drawer parts. Assemble the drawer fronts, sides, backs, and pulls with glue. While the glue is still wet, slide the bottoms in place — this will keep the drawers square while the glue cures. *Do not* glue the bottoms in the grooves; they must remain free to expand and contract. To keep them in place, tack the bottoms to the drawer backs with ¾" brads, as shown in the *Bottom Drawer Details/Side View.*

Allow the glue to cure overnight. Then sand and plane the drawer assemblies to fit the case. They should slide in and out smoothly, without binding.

TRY THIS! If you're building this project in the summer, fit the drawer assemblies very close to the case with almost no slop. If you're making it in the winter, allow a ¹⁄₁₆" gap between the drawers and the case; when the summer comes, the drawers will swell slightly and the gap will disappear. What about spring and fall? Split the difference and fit the drawers with ¹⁄₃₂" gaps.

10 **Apply a finish.** Remove the drawers from the case and do any necessary touch-up sanding. Finish the case, applying as many coats to the inside as you do the outside. This ensures that the parts shrink and swell evenly, and helps to prevent the case from distorting. Finish the outside face of the drawer fronts, but not the other surfaces of the drawers. Traditionally, the insides of drawers are left unfinished so they will absorb moisture readily. This keeps the contents of the chest from mildewing.

Step-by-Step: Making a Table Saw Insert for Cutting Narrow Stock

When cutting very narrow or very small pieces on your table saw, you must take care not to let the stock fall between the table and the blade. The blade will bind and the workpiece may be ruined. Depending on the material you're cutting, the saw may shatter it and throw the splinters at you.

A commercial insert leaves a gap of ⅛"-¼" between the blade and the work surface — plenty of room to lose a small workpiece. To prevent this, make a special table insert for your saw that leaves almost no gap at all.

First, cut a scrap of hardwood or hardboard to the same shape and thickness as the metal insert that came with the saw. It should fit tightly enough in the insert opening that it will remain in place without vibrating loose. In addition, the wooden insert must be flush with the table. To make the insert to the precise dimensions needed, cut it a little oversize. Then sand the edges and the top until the insert fits the saw perfectly.

Mount the blade that you want to use with the insert. (You must always use the insert with the same blade that you used to make it.) Lower the arbor so the blade is beneath the surface of the table.

Place the wooden insert in the worktable. Turn on the saw, and slowly raise the blade to its full height above the table. The running blade will cut a long, narrow slot in the insert, only as wide as the blade itself. Use this insert (and blade) whenever you cut narrow stock or small parts.

Toy Soldiers

Toy soldiers have always been popular among children, but they became more so during the Industrial Revolution. This was not because society became more violent and warlike. It was because the toy soldiers became more numerous and affordable.

Before that time, soldier sets usually consisted of a few hand-carved pieces. There were few professional toymakers, and few toys. In most rural areas, children's playthings were limited to what they could fashion for themselves or what their parents had time to make for them. But by 1850, there were dozens of toy *manufacturers* — entrepreneurs who adapted new industrial production techniques to toymaking. Within a few decades, playthings that once had been precious became commonplace. Whole armies of inexpensive metal, paper, or wooden soldiers were available in every general store.

The soldiers shown are typical of wooden figures produced during this transition period between hand and machine production. Most of the parts — body, arms, and base — could be turned on a back lathe. This invention made a dozen duplicate spindles in the time it took a single experienced turner to make just one. However, individual craftsmen still assembled and decorated the soldiers.

There are two patterns shown, redcoats and bluecoats, so you can make two opposing armies. These are *not,* however, copies of Revolutionary War uniforms, despite the titles of the drawings. They are from two different eras and no particular country. This, too, was common for nineteenth-century toymakers. They often mixed times, styles, and national colors freely, creating armies of fancy rather than fact.

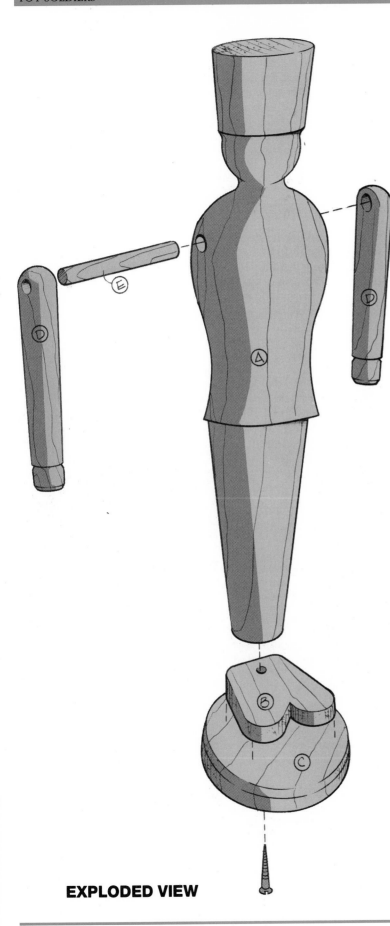

EXPLODED VIEW

Materials List

FINISHED DIMENSIONS

PARTS

A.	Body	1¾" dia. x 8⅜"
B.	Feet	¼" x 1¼" x 1½"
C.	Base	2" dia. x ½"
D.	Arms (2)	⅜" dia. x 3"
E.	Dowel	³⁄₁₆" dia. x 2½"

HARDWARE

#8 x 1½" Flathead wood screw

1 **_Select and prepare the stock._** Since each soldier will be painted, make it from light-colored stock. Fashion the body from a wood that's easy to turn, such as white pine. Make the other parts from harder woods, like maple or birch. You can use commercial hardwood dowel stock for the arms. All of these woods are fairly durable and provide a good painting surface.

The natural wood tones are almost white, so the colors that are painted over them remain vivid.

After selecting the stock, plane it to the thicknesses needed — ½" for the base and ¼" for the feet. Cut these parts to size. Make the arms and the ³⁄₁₆"-diameter dowel slightly longer than specified, and cut a 2" x 2" x 10" turning block for the body.

2 **_Make a turning template._** If you're making an army — even a small army — you want to make all the soldiers the same. To help do this, make a template from a scrap of ¼" plywood as shown in the *Turning Template* drawing. Cut the profile of a

soldier in one edge. If you're making soldiers from both the redcoat and bluecoat armies, cut both profiles — one in either edge. Transfer the measurements from the drawing to the template. These are the diameters of the high and the low spots on the body shapes.

3 **_Drill a hole in the body stock._** Lay the template against the body stock. Carefully mark the top and the bottom of the turning and the location

of the ³⁄₁₆"-diameter hole that passes through the chest. This hole holds a dowel that joins the arms to the soldier. Drill the hole through the block.

4 **_Turn the body shape._** Mount the block on a lathe and round it. Cut grooves to establish the diameters of the high and low spots. To turn a groove to a specific diameter, use a parting tool and calipers. Set the calipers to the proper measurement and hold them in one hand. With the other hand, place the parting tool against the turning. Slowly feed it into the wood, monitoring your progress with the calipers. As soon as they slip over the wood, stop turning. Cut grooves for each diameter along the length of the workpiece. (See Figure 1.)

Turn the shape of the soldier's body. Use the grooves as guides. When you cut the shape down to the bottom of a groove, stop there — you know you've reached the proper diameter. Some turners draw pencil lines on the bottom of each groove as a visual aid. When they start removing a pencil line, they know to stop cutting.

As the soldier takes shape, lay the template beside it now and then to check your progress. (See Figure 2.) Cut the contours on the turning to match those on the template. Don't worry about making them precisely the same; they just need to be close. The shape isn't critical, as long as each completed soldier looks like it's from the same army as the others.

1/Using calipers and a parting tool, turn grooves to specific diameters at the high and low spots along the soldier's body. These grooves will guide you as you turn the final shape.

2/As the turning takes shape, **turn off the lathe** every so often to compare the contours of the soldier and the template. Try to make them match.

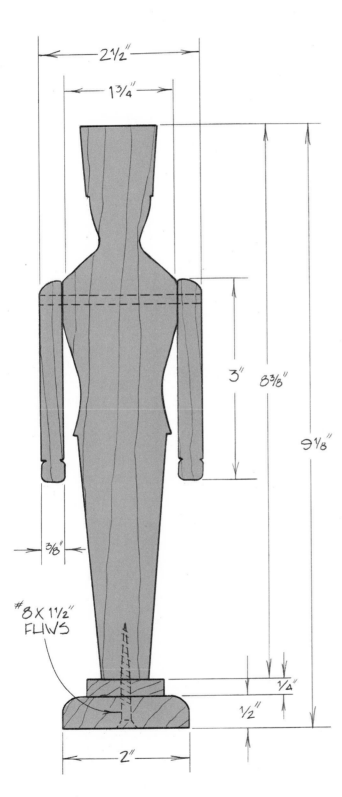

SOLDIER PROFILE

2½"

1¾"

3"

8⅜"

9⅛"

3/8"

#8 X 1½"
FLWS

¼"

½"

2"

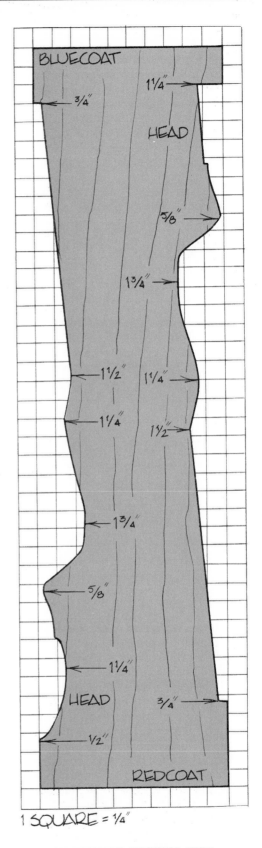

BLUECOAT

3/4"

1¼"

HEAD

5/8"

1¾"

1½"

1¼"

1¼"

1½"

1¾"

5/8"

1¼"

HEAD

3/4"

½"

REDCOAT

1 SQUARE = ¼"

TURNING TEMPLATE
(PRINTED AT 77%. ENLARGE ON
PHOTOCOPIER 1 TIME AT 129%.)

5

Turn the arms. If you're making the arms from ⅜"-diameter dowel stock, you'll find this is too small to mount between the centers of a lathe. Instead, mount a chuck accessory (either a lathe chuck or drill chuck) on the lathe's drive shaft, and clamp the dowel stock in the jaws of this chuck.

If you don't have a chuck accessory, you can use a drill press as a lathe. Make the jig shown in *Drill Press Turning Jig*. Clamp an arm piece in the chuck, and clamp the jig to the drill press table, directly beneath the arm piece. Using the point of a skew chisel, turn the hand at the end of the arm. (See Figure 3.) Repeat this procedure for the second arm.

3/Use a drill press lathe jig to turn the hands at the ends of the arms. This is easier and safer than turning them on a lathe. When mounting the arm pieces, be careful not to clamp them too tightly. You don't want the jaws of the chuck to mar the stock.

6

Make the feet and base. Transfer the *Feet Pattern* to the feet stock, and trace a 2"-diameter circle on the base stock. Cut out these shapes with a band saw or scroll saw. Sand the edges to remove saw marks.

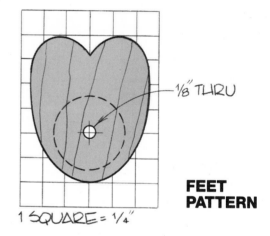

⅛" THRU

FEET PATTERN

1 SQUARE = ¼"

(PRINTED AT 100%.)

7

Assemble the feet, base, and body. Drill a ³⁄₁₆"-diameter shaft hole in the base, as shown in the *Base Layout*. Countersink this hole on the bottom of the base. Drill ⅛"-diameter pilot holes through the feet and just ¾" deep into the body, as shown on the *Feet Pattern* and the *Soldier Profile*.

Insert a #8 x 1½" flathead wood screw through the base from the bottom. Put glue on the bottom of the feet, and drive the screw through the feet. Draw the feet snug against the base. Put glue on the bottom end of the body, and turn the body onto the screw until the body is snug against the feet. Be careful to orient all three parts properly. You must center the feet on the base. They should face straight ahead, perpendicular to the dowel hole that runs side to side through the body.

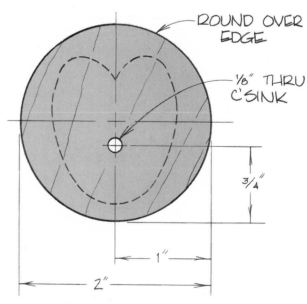

ROUND OVER EDGE

⅛" THRU C'SINK

¾"

1"

2"

BASE LAYOUT

8 **Attach the arms to the body.** Cut the arms to size, and drill a ³⁄₁₆"-diameter hole through each arm, near the top end. Insert the dowel through the ³⁄₁₆"-diameter hole in the body. Put glue on either end and attach the arms to the dowel. When the glue dries, sand or file the ends of the dowel flush with the arms.

> **TRY THIS!** If you want the arms to move, wax the *middle* of the dowel, where it passes through the body. *Don't* wax the ends. Poke holes in two small pieces of waxed paper, and slide them over the ends of the dowel. Glue the arms on the dowel. When the glue dries, tear off the pieces of paper. The arms will swing freely.

9 **Paint the soldier.** Round the top edges of the base and the feet with a chisel and a file. Finish sand all surfaces to prepare them for painting. (See Figure 4.) Draw a grid on the soldier and trace the *Front View, Side View,* and *Back View* patterns onto it. Make the grid lines very light; you don't want them to show through the paint.

Paint the soldier with latex or acrylic paint. Use the color codes on the drawings, or choose colors to suit your fancy. If you're making an army, paint all the soldiers at one time. Work assembly-line style, painting all the coats, then all the belts, then all the buttons, and so on. The uniforms will appear more homogeneous. And if you have to mix colors, they will be more consistent.

4/If you have one, use a flap sander to round the edges of the feet and base, and to smooth the contoured surfaces. Otherwise, sanding is apt to be a chore, especially if you're assembling several soldiers.

Variations

If you wish, your soldiers can each carry a rifle or sword. Trace the patterns on ⅛"-thick stock, and cut them out with a band saw or scroll saw. Glue the weapons directly to the right arm of each soldier, straight up and down.

Each weapon must be mounted so that the rifle butt or sword handle is even with the soldier's right hand.

(PRINTED AT 100%.)

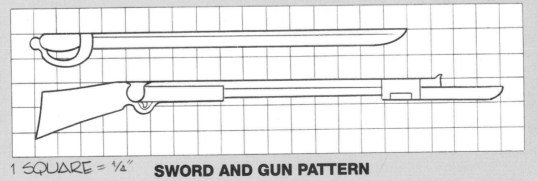

1 SQUARE = ¼"   **SWORD AND GUN PATTERN**

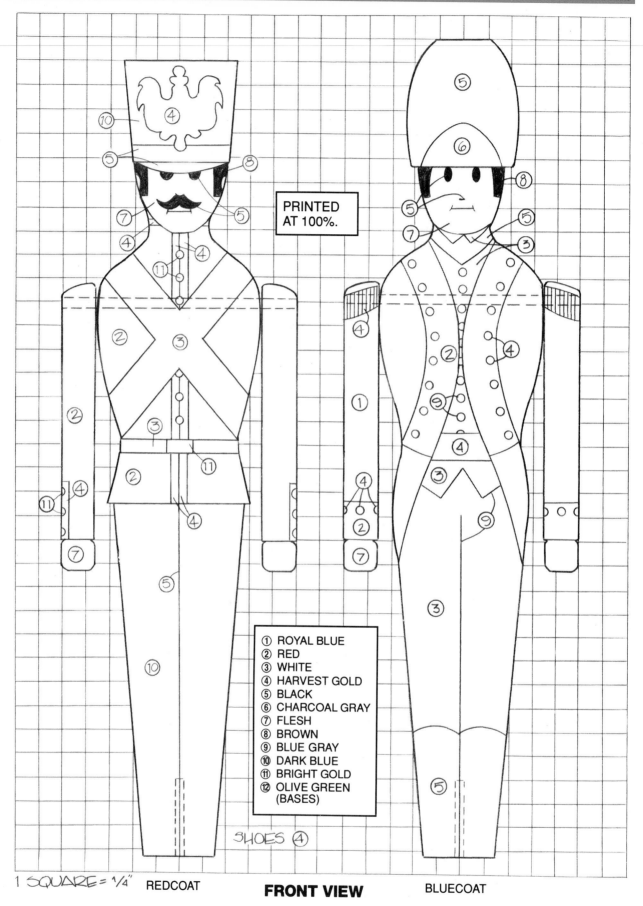

PRINTED
AT 100%.

① ROYAL BLUE
② RED
③ WHITE
④ HARVEST GOLD
⑤ BLACK
⑥ CHARCOAL GRAY
⑦ FLESH
⑧ BROWN
⑨ BLUE GRAY
⑩ DARK BLUE
⑪ BRIGHT GOLD
⑫ OLIVE GREEN
   (BASES)

SHOES ④

1 SQUARE = ¼"   REDCOAT   **FRONT VIEW**   BLUECOAT

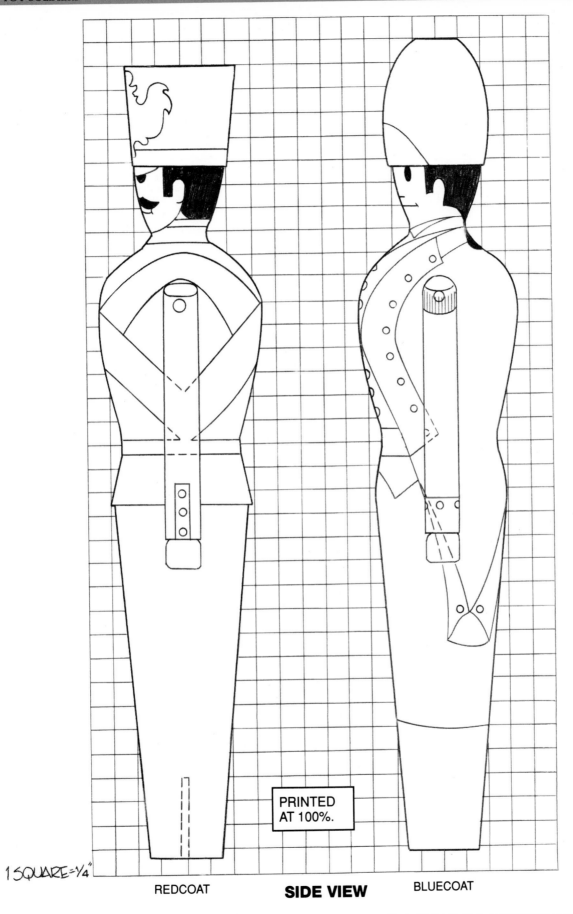

1 SQUARE = ¼"

REDCOAT **SIDE VIEW** BLUECOAT

PRINTED
AT 100%.

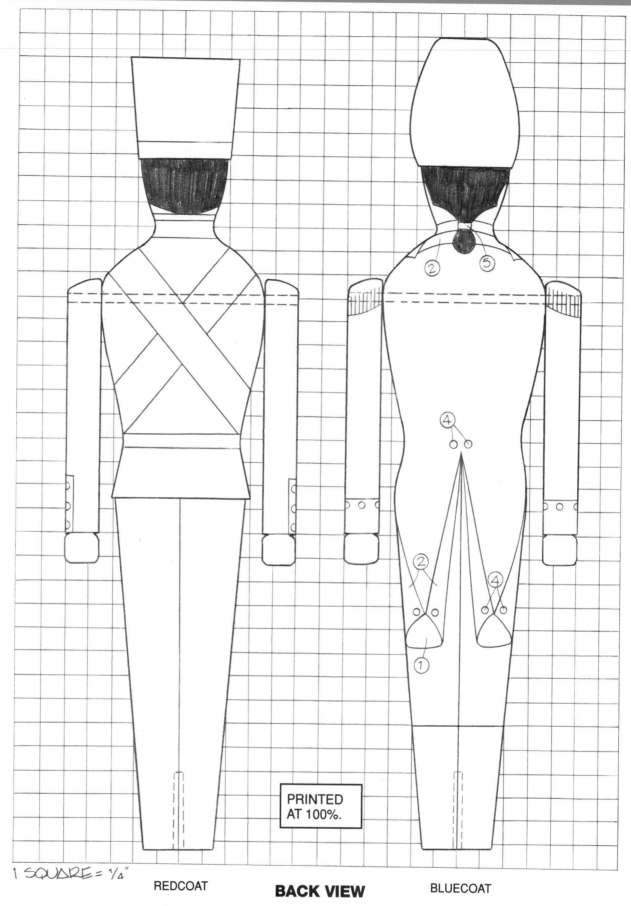

1 SQUARE = ¼"

REDCOAT

BACK VIEW

BLUECOAT

PRINTED
AT 100%.

Noah's Ark

Sunday was a day of rest for country folk — not just for grown-ups, but for the whole family. To discourage boisterous activity on the Sabbath, parents made special toys for their children. These "Sunday toys," as they were called, kept the kids peacefully occupied for the day. A miniature ark, filled with animals, was an especially popular plaything. Not only did it inspire quiet play; it was educational and had a biblical theme.

Arks still make wonderful toys for precisely the same reasons. They also appeal to big kids — homespun arks with sets of hand-painted animals are prized by collectors of folk art. Perhaps more than any other rustic artifact, they speak to us of the simple joys of country life.

The ark shown is just a small box — a toy box, actually — painted and decorated to look like a boat. One half of the cabin roof and a section of hull are hinged so you can store animals inside. The animals are simple cutouts, simply painted. The edges are rounded over, and some can be rough-carved to create ears, tusks, tails, and so on. But none are finely shaped or finished. Children (both large and small) must fill in the details with their imaginations.

Note: To make this project easier to re-create, all the animal patterns in this chapter are full-size. You don't have to enlarge them!

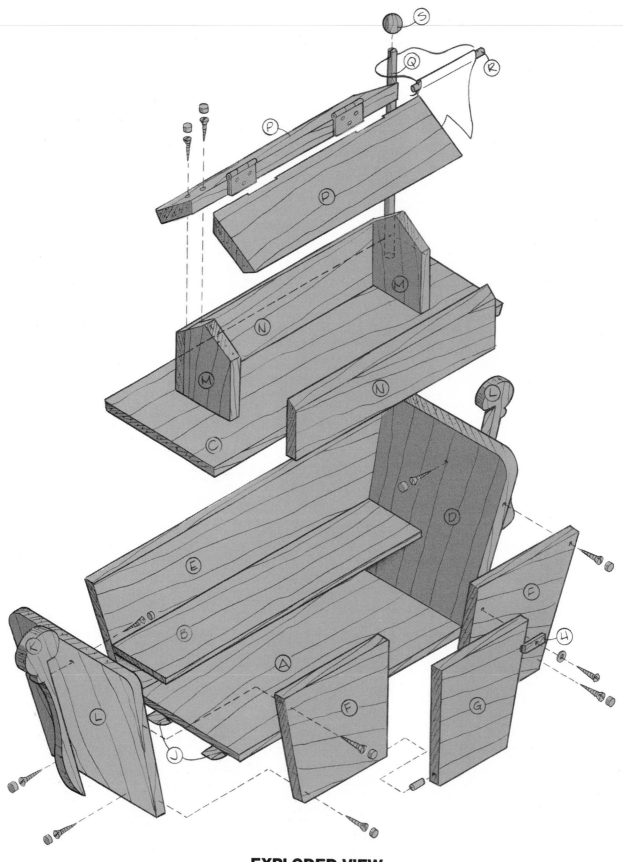

EXPLODED VIEW

Materials List

FINISHED DIMENSIONS

PARTS

Ark

A.	Bottom	$\frac{1}{2}$" x $5^{15}/_{16}$" x $12^{5}/_{16}$"
B.	Mid deck	$\frac{1}{2}$" x $2\frac{3}{4}$" x $13^{15}/_{16}$"
C.	Top deck	$\frac{1}{2}$" x $6^{15}/_{16}$" x $15\frac{3}{8}$"
D.	Bow/stern (2)	$\frac{1}{2}$" x 7" x $7\frac{5}{8}$"
E.	Starboard side	$\frac{1}{2}$" x $6\frac{5}{8}$" x $16\frac{5}{8}$"
F.	Port side halves (2)	$\frac{1}{2}$" x $6\frac{5}{8}$" x $5\frac{3}{4}$"
G.	Loading ramp	$\frac{1}{2}$" x 5" x $6\frac{5}{8}$"
H.	Latch	$\frac{1}{4}$" x $\frac{1}{2}$" x $1\frac{1}{4}$"
J.	Runners (2)	$\frac{1}{4}$" x $\frac{1}{2}$" x $12\frac{3}{4}$"
K.	Bowsprit	$\frac{1}{2}$" x $2\frac{1}{4}$" x $8\frac{3}{4}$"
L.	Rudder	$\frac{1}{2}$" x $1\frac{7}{8}$" x $8\frac{3}{8}$"
M.	Cabin ends (2)	$\frac{1}{2}$" x 3" x 4"
N.	Cabin port/starboard sides (2)	$\frac{1}{2}$" x $3\frac{1}{8}$" x 10"
P.	Roof halves (2)	$\frac{1}{2}$" x 3" x $11\frac{1}{2}$"
Q.	Mast	$\frac{5}{16}$" dia. x $8\frac{3}{4}$"
R.	Spar	$\frac{1}{4}$" dia. x $2\frac{1}{2}$"
S.	Bead	$\frac{1}{2}$" dia.

Animals

A.	Elephants (2)	$\frac{3}{4}$" x $4\frac{1}{2}$" x $4\frac{3}{4}$"
B.	Giraffes (2)	$\frac{3}{4}$" x $2\frac{3}{4}$" x $4\frac{3}{4}$"
C.	Camels (2)	$\frac{3}{4}$" x $2\frac{5}{8}$" x $3\frac{1}{8}$"
D.	Cattle (2)	$\frac{3}{4}$" x $2\frac{7}{8}$" x 4"
E.	Zebras (2)	$\frac{3}{4}$" x $3\frac{1}{8}$" x $3\frac{1}{4}$"
F.	Lion	$\frac{3}{4}$" x $2\frac{3}{8}$" x $4\frac{3}{4}$"
G.	Lioness	$\frac{3}{4}$" x $2\frac{1}{8}$" x $4\frac{3}{4}$"
H.	Tigers (2)	$\frac{3}{4}$" x $1\frac{7}{8}$" x 4"
J.	Elk (buck)	$\frac{3}{4}$" x $3\frac{1}{8}$" x $3\frac{1}{2}$"
K.	Elk (doe)	$\frac{3}{4}$" x $2\frac{7}{8}$" x $2\frac{7}{8}$"
L.	Bears (2)	$\frac{3}{4}$" x $2\frac{1}{8}$" x 3"
M.	Ram	$\frac{3}{4}$" x $1\frac{3}{4}$" x $2\frac{3}{8}$"
N.	Ewe	$\frac{3}{4}$" x $1\frac{5}{8}$" x $2\frac{1}{4}$"
P.	Swans (2)	$\frac{3}{4}$" x $1\frac{7}{8}$" x 2"
Q.	Rooster	$\frac{1}{2}$" x $1\frac{1}{2}$" x $1\frac{3}{4}$"
R.	Hen	$\frac{1}{2}$" x $1\frac{1}{8}$" x $1\frac{5}{8}$"
S.	Noah	$\frac{3}{4}$" x $1\frac{3}{4}$" x $3\frac{1}{8}$"
T.	Esther	$\frac{3}{4}$" x $1\frac{1}{8}$" x 3"

HARDWARE

Ark

#8 x $1\frac{1}{4}$" Flathead wood screws (30–36)

#6 x $\frac{5}{8}$" Roundhead wood screw and flat washer

$\frac{1}{2}$" Wire brads (6–8)

$\frac{3}{16}$" dia. x 1" Metal pins (2)

$1\frac{1}{4}$" x $1\frac{1}{2}$" Butt hinges and mounting screws (1 pair)

Canvas or aluminum flashing ($2\frac{1}{4}$" x 3")

Twine (4")

Animals

#10 Copper wire (4")

Making the Ark

1 **Select the stock and cut it to size.** Arks were commonly made from durable, light-colored woods, such as maple or birch. These stand up well to the abuse that children dish out even during quiet play. If you are making this project for show rather than play, you can consider a wider range of woods — white pine, soft maple, almost any near-white wood. (The ark shown was made from poplar.) All of these provide a light surface that will not dull or change the paint colors.

After selecting the stock, plane it $\frac{1}{2}$" thick. (You can cut all the parts for the ark itself from a single stock thickness; those listed as $\frac{1}{4}$" thick on the Materials List happen to be $\frac{1}{2}$" wide.) Cut the parts to the sizes shown, with the exceptions listed below. Note that you must bevel-cut many of the parts. Also, note that the ark, like any boat, has four distinct sides — bow (or front), stern (back), port (left), and starboard (right). These are referred to often in the instructions:

■ Bevel the bottom edge of the *bow* and *stern* at 15°. Cut them about $\frac{1}{8}$" wider than specified.

■ Bevel the ends (bow and stern) of the *bottom* and the *top deck* at 15°, and the edges (port and starboard) at 5°. Cut both parts about $\frac{1}{8}$" wider than specified.

■ Bevel the ends (bow and stern) of the *mid deck* at 15°, and the starboard edge at 5°. (The port edge should be square.) Cut this part about $\frac{1}{16}$" wider than specified.

■ Bevel the top edges of the *cabin port side* and *cabin starboard* side at 30°. Cut them to the dimensions specified.

■ Bevel the adjoining edges of the *roof halves* at 30°. Cut them to the dimensions specified.

2 Cut the patterns and special shapes.
Cut the shapes of the bowsprit, rudder, bow, stern, and cabin ends:

■ Taper the sides of the *bow* and *stern* at 5°, using a table saw and a tapering jig. (After you cut the tapers, these parts should still be approximately ⅛" wider than shown in the Materials List.) Round the top corners, as shown on the *Bow/Stern Layout*, with a sander.

■ Enlarge the *Bowsprit and Rudder Patterns*, and transfer them onto the stock. Cut them out with a band saw or scroll saw. Pay careful attention to the grain direction! Sand the edges to remove the saw marks.

■ Measure and mark the gable shape on the *cabin ends* as shown in the *Back (Stern) View*. Cut these parts on a table saw or radial arm saw.

3 Finish sand the parts.
Finish sand all the parts of the ark to prepare them for assembly. Be careful not to round any of the edges. Otherwise, some of the joints may gap when you put the ark together.

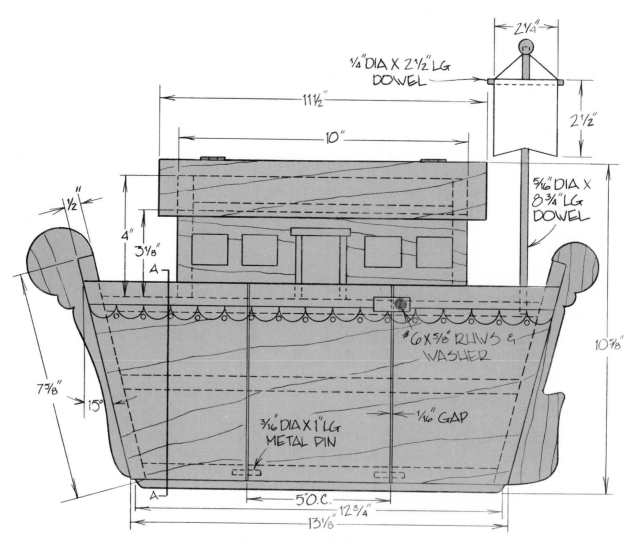

LEFT SIDE (PORT) VIEW

4

Assemble the roof halves. Mortise the halves of the cabin roof for butt hinges. These mortises are simple, shallow notches cut in the beveled edges. You can make them with a chisel, dado cutter, or table-mounted router, whichever you prefer. Tem-porarily install the hinges, joining the roof parts. When the hinges are closed, the beveled edges of the roof halves must be flush with one another, as shown in the *Back (Stern) View*.

5

Assemble the cabin. Glue the cabin port side and starboard side to the cabin ends. When the glue dries, sand all the surfaces clean and flush. Set the roof assembly atop the cabin assembly and center it. The roof should overhang ¾" on either end, as shown in the *Left Side (Port) View*.

Glue and screw the *starboard* half of the roof to the cabin, counterboring and countersinking the screws.

(Leave the port half unattached, so you can raise and lower it, like the lid of a box.) Glue short lengths of dowel in the counterbores to cover the screw heads. Remove the hinges and the port half of the roof (so it won't be flopping open and shut during the next few steps). Sand the dowel ends flush with the roof surface. The roof will look as if it's doweled in place.

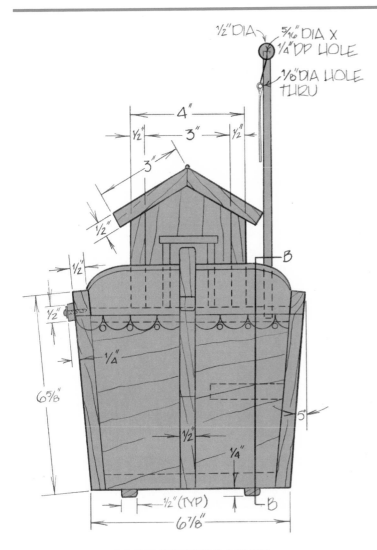

BACK (STERN) VIEW

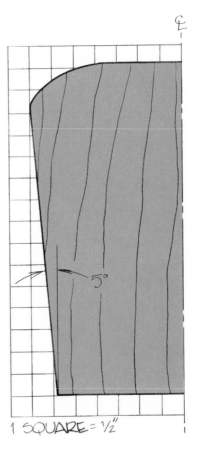

BOW/STERN LAYOUT

(PRINTED AT 46%.
ENLARGE 3 TIMES ON
PHOTOCOPIER AT 129%.)

6

Attach the cabin to the top deck. Drill a 5/16"-diameter, 3/8"-deep hole in the top deck to mount the mast, as shown in the *Top View*. Center the cabin on the top deck and mark the position of all four corners. Drill four 1/8"-diameter pilot holes through the deck, just inside the corner marks. Attach the cabin to the deck with glue and screws, driving the screws up through the 1/8"-diameter holes in the deck. Countersink the screws, but don't bother to counterbore or cover the heads — you won't see them when you assemble the ark.

7

Attach the bowsprit and rudder. Center the bowsprit on the bow, and the rudder on the stern. Glue the parts in place, then reinforce them with screws driven from inside the ark. Use just one screw to hold the bowsprit, near the top. Use two screws to hold the rudder, one near the top and the other near the bottom. Counterbore and countersink the top screws, then cover the heads. Otherwise, they will show when you assemble the ark. Simply countersink the bottom screw — it won't be seen.

8

Assemble the ark. To make a "tight ship," you must assemble the parts of the ark in a specific order, hand-fitting them as you work. Begin at the bottom. Attach the bow and the stern assemblies to the bottom with screws and glue. Counterbore and countersink the screws, then cover the heads. (Do this for *all* screws from here on, unless otherwise indicated.)

Attach the top and mid decks to the bow and stern with glue and screws. The starboard edge of the mid deck should be flush with the starboard edges of the bow and stern. Both decks should be parallel with the bottom, as shown in *Section A* and *Section B*.

Allow the glue to dry, then sand the *starboard* edges clean and flush. This is very important! Because all four sides of the ark are slanted, the edges of the bow and stern must be sanded to compound angles. (This is why you made several parts slightly wider than shown in the Materials List — so you'd have some extra stock to grind away.) If you don't do this, the sides won't fit properly.

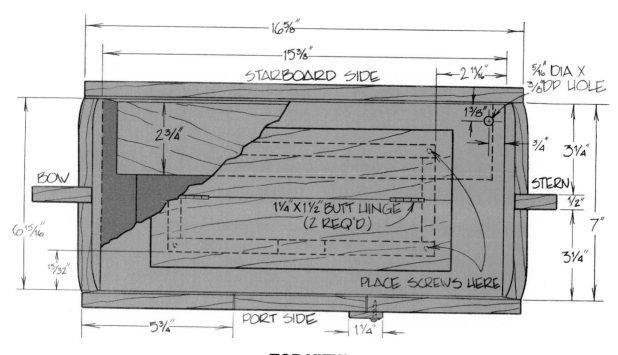

TOP VIEW

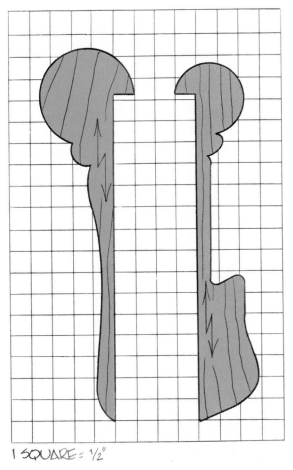

1 SQUARE = 1/2"

BOWSPRIT AND RUDDER PATTERNS

(PRINTED AT 46%. ENLARGE
3 TIMES ON PHOTOCOPIER AT 129%.)

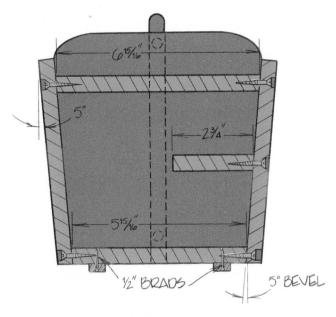

6 15/16"

5°

2 3/4"

5 15/16"

1/2" BRADS

5° BEVEL

SECTION A

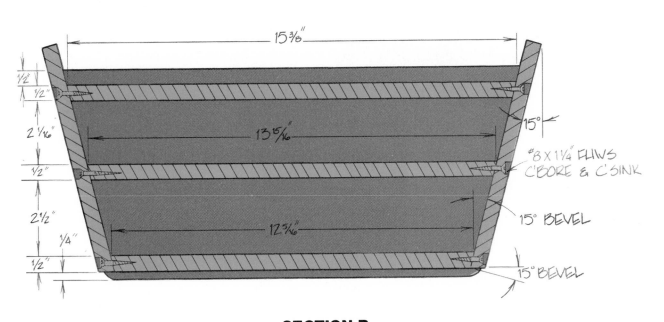

15 3/8"

1/2"

1/2"

2 1/16"

13 15/16"

1/2"

2 1/2"

12 5/16"

1/4"

1/2"

15°

#8 X 1 1/4" FHWS
C'BORE & C'SINK

15° BEVEL

15° BEVEL

SECTION B

Use a stationary disk or belt sander, if you have it, to do the sanding. Tilt the worktable to 85°, turn the sander on, and gently press the ark assembly against the sanding surface. (See Figure 1.) Keep the ark moving, and be careful not to sand one spot more than another. Periodically check your work by holding the starboard side against the assembly. When it fits flush, with no gaps in any of the seams, stop sanding.

If you don't have a stationary sander, cut a scrap of ¾" plywood, about 9" wide and 18" long. Using spray adhesive or contact cement, attach several sheets of 80# sandpaper to the good side (the side with no voids) of the board. Butt the sheets edge to edge on the board. They shouldn't overlap, but allow no gaps between them. Secure this sanding jig to your workbench and place the ark assembly on the sandpaper, starboard side down. Slide the ark back and forth, sanding the starboard edges flush. This will take some time, but it's actually more accurate than using a power sander.

1/To attach the sides to the ark, with no gaps at the seams, sand the edges of the assembly. This will ensure that all the adjoining edges are flush, clean, and properly beveled.

Glue and screw the starboard side to the ark. Screw the port side pieces as well, but don't glue them to the assembly or cover the screws. You need to remove the pieces in the next step.

9

Install the ramp on the ark. Fit the loading ramp between the port side pieces. It should fit with just enough room to open and close without binding. If it's too tight, sand some stock from the edges. If it's too loose, make another ramp.

Remove the port side pieces from the ark. Carefully mark and drill ³⁄₁₆"-diameter holes, ½"-deep, near the bottom inside corners, as shown in the *Ramp Pivot Detail* and *Left Side (Port) View*. Round the inside bottom corner of the ramp, so it will pivot without binding. (See Figure 2.)

Cut 1"-long pins from ³⁄₁₆"-diameter metal bar stock to make the ramp pivots. Place these pivots in the holes you drilled in the side pieces. Screw one of the side pieces to the ark assembly; put the ramp in place; then screw the other piece to the ark.

Check the action of the ramp. It should swing open and shut freely. If it binds, loosen one side piece and remove the ramp. Sand a little more stock from the bottom corner and reinstall the parts. Once the ramp works properly, remove all the parts from the port side. Reassemble the side pieces with glue and screws. Be careful not to get any glue on the ramp — it must pivot freely. Cover the screw heads.

2/If you have a stationary disk sander, use it to round the inside bottom corner of the ramp. Gently press the bottom of the ramp against the sander while raising and lowering the top. Be careful to remove the same amount of stock all along the corner.

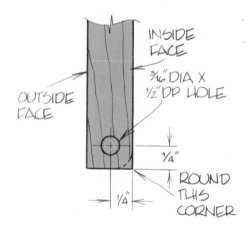

RAMP PIVOT DETAIL

10 Attach the latch, runners, and roof.

Sand all the joints clean and flush. Cut off the dowels covering the screw heads as close to the surface as possible. Sand them flush.

Drill a ⅛"-diameter hole in the latch. Place the latch on either of the port side pieces, near the top edge. Position it so it keeps the ramp up when the latch is horizontal. Drive a roundhead screw with washer through the latch and into the side, as shown in the *Left Side (Port) View* and *Back (Stern) View*. Tighten the screw so it's snug, but not so snug that you can't turn the latch easily.

Most old-time arks had runners. This made it easier for children to scoot them across a floor or a carpet. On this project, the runners also keep the ramp from rubbing on the floor when it is raised or lowered. Round the ends of these runners as you did the corner of the ramp. Glue the runners to the bottom of the ark and tack them in place with brads. After the glue dries, set the heads of the brads.

Place the port half of the roof back on the cabin. Attach it to the starboard half with the hinges you installed previously.

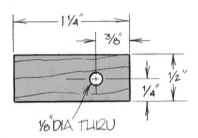

LATCH DETAIL

11 Make and install the mast.

Drill a ⁵⁄₁₆"-diameter, ¼"-deep hole in the bead. The easiest way to get a small bead to lie still when you're drilling it is to make a cradle for it. In a piece of scrap wood, bore a hole slightly smaller than the diameter of the bead. Place the bead in the hole to drill it. The pressure of the bit will keep the bead in the hole while you work. (See Figure 3.)

Drill ⅛"-diameter holes through the mast and the spar, placed where shown in the *Back (Stern) View*. Cut a piece of canvas or aluminum flashing for the banner, as shown in the *Left Side (Port) View*. If you're using canvas, hem the edges and sew a casing in the top. Insert the spar through this casing. If you're using flashing, simply bend the thin aluminum over the spar.

Warning: If you're making the ark for small children, *don't use aluminum flashing* for the banner. They may cut themselves on the sharp edges. Use the canvas instead, even though it requires more work.

Hang the banner on the mast. Tie a knot in one end of a short length of twine. Thread the twine up through one of the ⅛"-diameter holes in the spar, through the hole in the mast, and down through the other hole in the spar. Tie a knot in the other end of the twine so it won't slip out of the holes, and trim the loose ends.

Finally, glue the bead to the top of the mast. *Don't glue the mast in the deck; just insert it in the mounting hole. You (or your children) may wish to remove the mast assembly when the ark is in storage. The mast will fit inside the hull with the animals.

3/Drill a small hole in a scrap and rest the bead in it while drilling. If the bead wants to spin in the hole, apply contact cement to the rim.

12 *Paint the ark.* Do any necessary touch-up sanding on the ark. Round over all the hard corners and edges, then rub it down with a tack cloth to remove any sanding dust.

Coat the banner with sizing, if you've made it from canvas. Sizing makes the canvas less porous, so it's easier to paint. It's available at arts-and-crafts stores. If you made the banner from aluminum, apply zinc chromate primer. When the sizing or priming coat dries, transfer the *Banner Pattern* to both sides of the banner. Don't prime any wood surfaces — the paint adheres better to raw wood, and also covers well.

Paint the ark with latex or acrylic paint. Both of these are nontoxic (after they dry) and they dry quickly. Follow the color coding on the drawings, or choose your own colors.

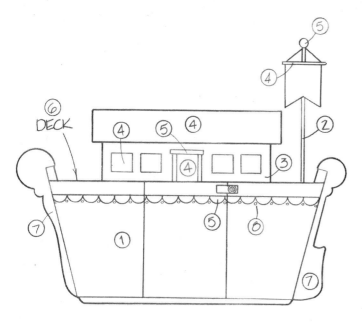

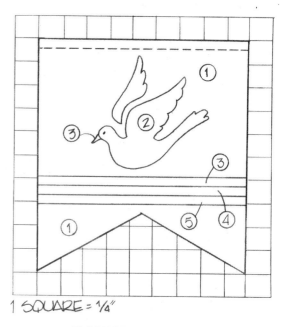

ARK COLOR CHART

① KELLY GREEN
② MEDIUM BLUE
③ DARK BLUE
④ RUST ORANGE
⑤ PEACH
⑥ LIGHT PEACH
⑦ LIGHT GREEN
⑧ LIGHT BLUE

BANNER PATTERN

(PRINTED AT 100%.)

① DARK BLUE
② WHITE
③ PEACH
④ LIGHT BLUE
⑤ MEDIUM BLUE

Making the Animals

13 *Select and prepare the stock.* Like the ark, the animals should be made from a durable, light-colored wood. This wood should also be easy to cut, and carve. Basswood is your best choice, followed by butternut and lauan mahogany. For more information on choosing woods for carving, see the introductory chapter, Chust for So.

Whatever wood you select, you'll have to make it a little stronger before you can use it. Many of the animals in the ark have appendages sticking out at odd angles. Some of these appendages will be very fragile if you make the animals from solid wood. For example, if you orient the grain of the wood along the body of the lion, the legs will be weak. If you run the grain along the neck of the giraffe, the nose may break off.

To solve this problem, make your own *plywood*. Use a band saw to resaw the wood into ¼"-thick sheets. Glue up ¾"-thick stock (three sheets joined face to face), with the grain of each sheet perpendicular to the adjoining sheet. You need very little. Just 1½ to 2 square feet of ¾"-thick homemade plywood is enough to make all the animals (and people) shown in the patterns.

Note: You can use the ¾" plywood for the rooster and chicken; there's no need to make up a special piece of ½" plywood for these two small animals. After you make the ¾" plywood, cut a small section off one end and resaw it to ½" thick.

14 Cut the animal shapes.
Transfer the animal patterns to the plywood, and cut the shapes with a scroll saw or a band saw. If you use a band saw, work with a ⅛"-wide or ¹⁄₁₆"-wide blade. Cut as much of each animal shape as you can in a normal manner, then use the blade to nibble away the waste in areas that are too small to turn the blade. (See Figure 4.)

4/You can cut very intricate shapes on a band saw by nibbling away the waste instead of cutting. To nibble with a band saw, use the teeth of the blade as a tiny rasp, carefully pressing the stock against them.

15 Round the edges of the animals.
You needn't carve the animals — many Noah's Ark animal sets were simple silhouettes. Just round the edges to soften their appearance and make the animals look time-worn. Use a carving knife to remove all the hard edges *except* the bottom edges. These should remain flat, so the animals will stand upright.

If you have the time and the patience, rough-carve some of the larger details such as the lion's mane, the elephants' ears, the swans' necks, and so on. (See Figure 5.) These needn't be realistic. In fact, they shouldn't be. A country craftsman usually wouldn't have the time or the skill to make tiny, realistic sculptures. Even if he did, he wouldn't make them for children to play with. Your carving should just suggest the three-dimensional shape of the animal.

5/If you wish, rough-carve some of the larger details in the animals to make them appear more three-dimensional.

16 **Sand the animals.** After you round (and perhaps carve) the animals, sand them to remove all saw and knife marks. You can speed this chore with a flap sander. (See Figure 6.) This inexpensive drill press accessory is a plastic or metal hub with strips of sandpaper attached to it. Mount the hub in the chuck and run the drill press at medium or low speed. Hold an animal shape against the whirling sanding strips, turning it this way and that. The strips reach into the cracks and crevices like sandpaper fingers, smoothing even the recessed areas of the animal.

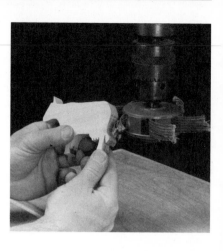

6/A flap sander quickly smooths complex three-dimensional shapes. These come in many different grits. Use 120# or higher, so you don't remove too much stock too fast.

ELK
① TAN
② MEDIUM BROWN
③ IVORY

NOAH
① HARVEST GOLD
② GOLD BROWN
③ GREEN
④ WHITE
⑤ DARK BROWN
⑥ FLESH

1 SQUARE = 1/2"

ANIMAL PATTERNS

17

Make Noah's crook. Noah's crook is too thin and too fragile to be made from wood — even plywood. Instead, make this tiny piece from a scrap of copper wire. Put a tight bend at the end of a short length of 10-gauge wire. Drill a ⅛"-diameter hole through Noah's hand and insert the wire crook. Keep it in place with epoxy glue.

18

Paint the animals. Color the animals (and the people) with the same latex or acrylic paint you used to finish the ark. Follow the suggested colors. Or, if you wish, go to the library and take out some picture books of animals. Use these to guide you as you paint.

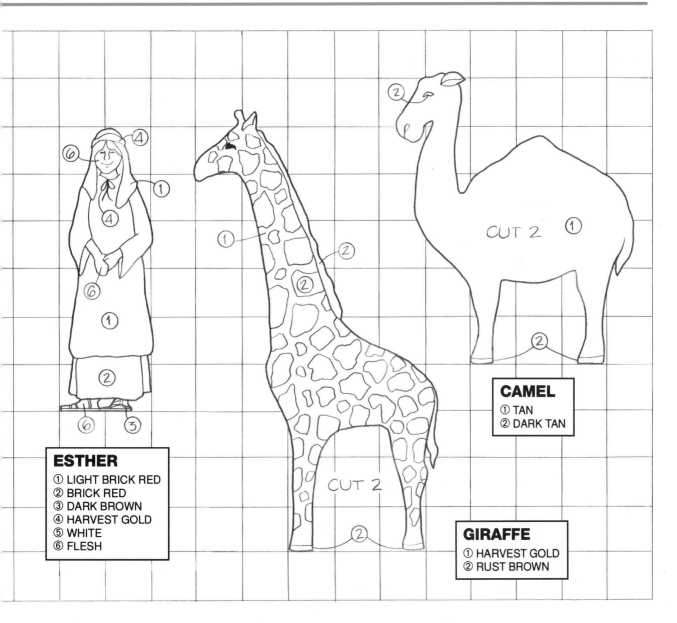

ESTHER
① LIGHT BRICK RED
② BRICK RED
③ DARK BROWN
④ HARVEST GOLD
⑤ WHITE
⑥ FLESH

CAMEL
① TAN
② DARK TAN

GIRAFFE
① HARVEST GOLD
② RUST BROWN

CUT 2

(PRINTED AT 100%.)

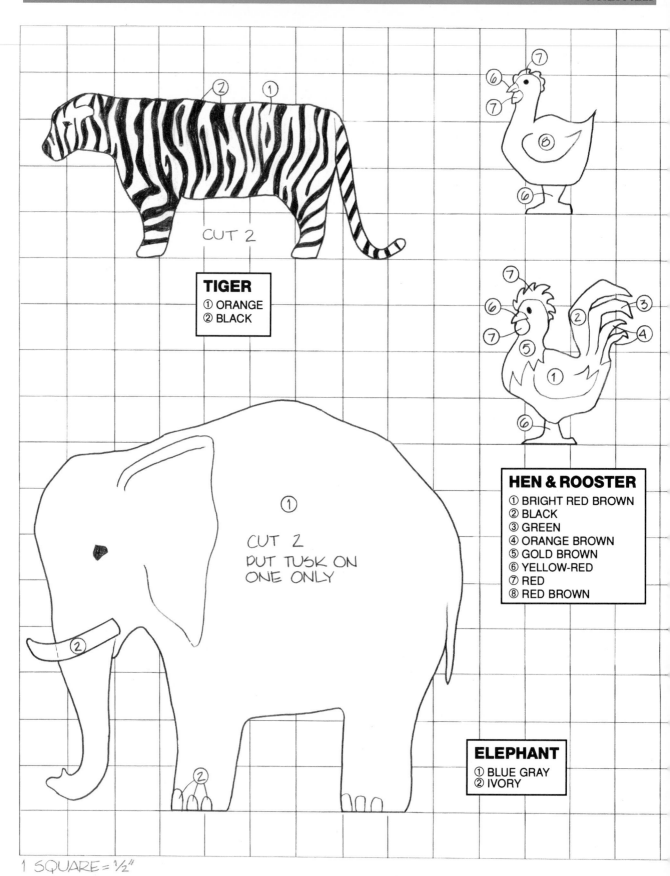

CUT 2

TIGER
① ORANGE
② BLACK

HEN & ROOSTER
① BRIGHT RED BROWN
② BLACK
③ GREEN
④ ORANGE BROWN
⑤ GOLD BROWN
⑥ YELLOW-RED
⑦ RED
⑧ RED BROWN

CUT 2
PUT TUSK ON
ONE ONLY

ELEPHANT
① BLUE GRAY
② IVORY

1 SQUARE = ½"

ANIMAL PATTERNS

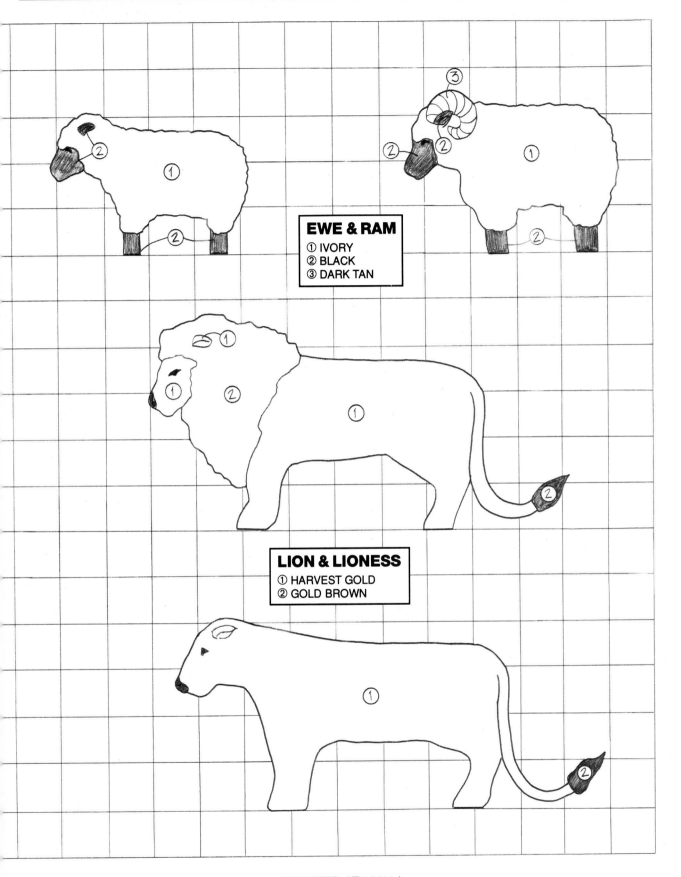

EWE & RAM
① IVORY
② BLACK
③ DARK TAN

LION & LIONESS
① HARVEST GOLD
② GOLD BROWN

(PRINTED AT 100%.)

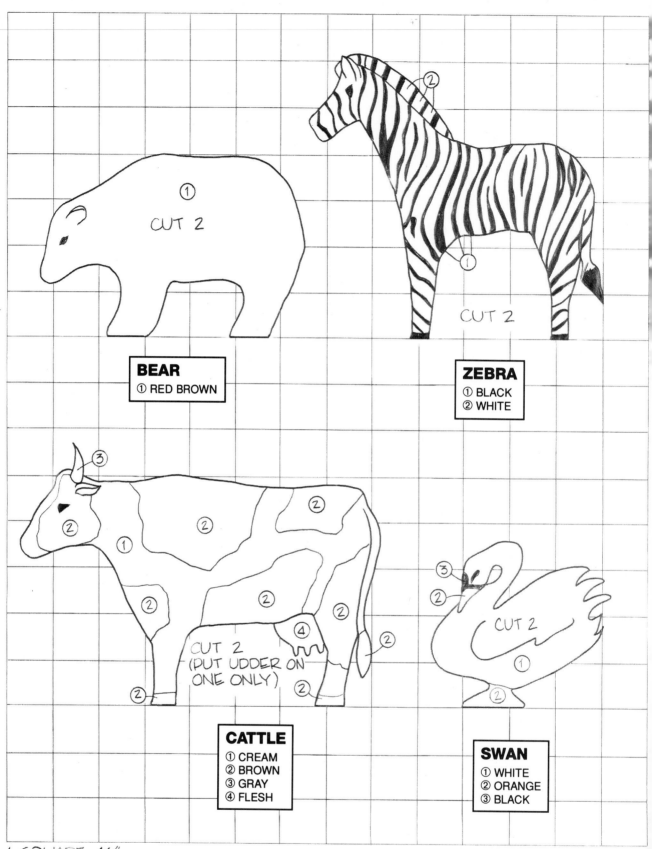

BEAR
① RED BROWN

ZEBRA
① BLACK
② WHITE

CATTLE
① CREAM
② BROWN
③ GRAY
④ FLESH

SWAN
① WHITE
② ORANGE
③ BLACK

CUT 2

CUT 2

CUT 2
(PUT UDDER ON ONE ONLY)

CUT 2

1 SQUARE = ½"

(PRINTED AT 100%.)

Credits

Contributing Craftsmen and Craftswomen:

Dick Belcher (Pull Toys, Butter Press)

Nick Engler (Adjustable Candlestand, Toy Wagon, Shaker Peg Rail and Clothes Hangers)

Mary Jane Favorite (Noah's Ark, Pull Toys, Miniature Rocking Horse, Door Harp, Toy Soldiers, Bird Decoys, Toy Wagon, Barn Signs)

Rude Osolnik (Burled Bowls and Cups)

Larry Owrey (Shaker Oval Boxes, Shaker Peg Rail and Clothes Hangers)

Robert S. Pinter (Burled Bowls and Cups)

Note: One project, the Miniature Chest of Drawers, was built by a country craftsman whose name has been erased by time. We regret that we cannot tell you who built it; we can only admire his (or her) craftsmanship.

The designs for the newer projects in this book (those attributed to a designer or builder) are the copyrighted property of the craftsmen and craftswomen who built them. Readers are encouraged to reproduce these projects for their personal use or for gifts. However, reproduction for sale or profit is forbidden by law.

Special Thanks To:
Mr. and Mrs. Nicholas Engler, Jr.
Gordon Honeyman
Wertz Hardware Stores, West Milton, Ohio

Rodale Press, Inc., publishes AMERICAN WOODWORKER™, the magazine for the serious woodworking hobbyist. For information on how to order your subscription, write to AMERICAN WOODWORKER™, Emmaus, PA 18098.

WOODWORKING GLOSSARY

Parts of a Board

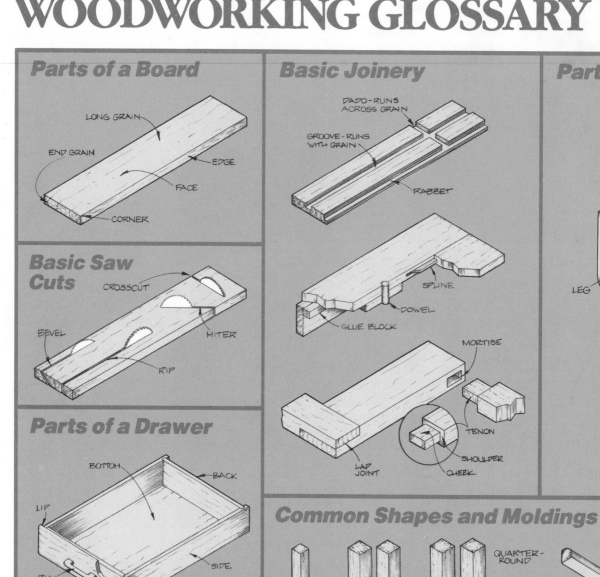

LONG GRAIN

END GRAIN

EDGE

FACE

CORNER

Basic Saw Cuts

CROSSCUT

BEVEL

MITER

RIP

Parts of a Drawer

BOTTOM

BACK

LIP

SIDE

PULL

FACE

FRONT

Parts of a Frame

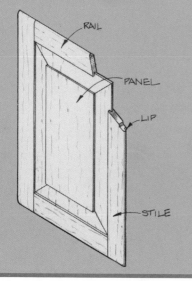

RAIL

PANEL

LIP

STILE

Basic Joinery

DADO - RUNS ACROSS GRAIN

GROOVE - RUNS WITH GRAIN

RABBET

SPLINE

DOWEL

GLUE BLOCK

MORTISE

TENON

LAP JOINT

SHOULDER

CHEEK

Parts of a T...

LEAF

LEG

KNEE

ANKLE

FOOT

Common Shapes and Moldings

QUARTER-ROUND

BEAD

OGEE, OR CYMA CURVE

CORNER

COVE

BED

CROWN

CABRIOLE

TAPER

STRAIGHT

Holes

SCREW HOLE

STOPPED HOLE

THRU HOLE

COUNTERBORE

COUNTERSINK

PILOT HOLE

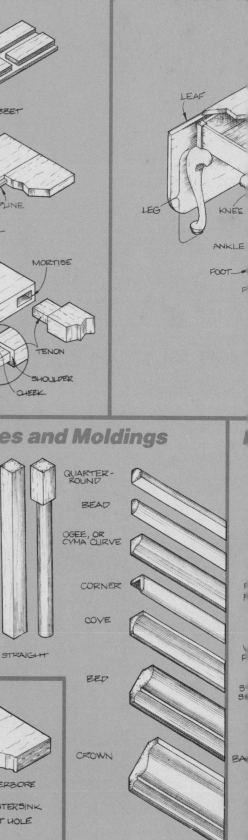

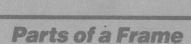